Teachers' Guide to American Negro History

TEACHERS' GUIDE
TO
AMERICAN NEGRO
HISTORY

by
William Loren Katz

Revised Edition

Quadrangle Books
Chicago

To my great teachers—
Kenneth Haskins, Sara Jackson,
Ernest Kaiser, and Bernard Katz

FIRST EDITION 1968, FIVE PRINTINGS
SECOND EDITION, REVISED, 1971

Although the Negro has played a significant role in history since the dawn of civilization, his contributions have been ignored by historians and his face has rarely appeared in history texts. Even Paul Revere's famous drawing of the Boston Massacre portrays a battle among whites, despite the fact that Negroes were present and one leader, Crispus Attucks, was among the five American martyrs. Historian Benson J. Lossing transformed Attucks into a "Nantucket Indian."

The distortion of the Negro's past has always had a purpose. The assertion that the Negro has no history worth mentioning is basic to the theory that he has no humanity worth defending. Deliberate misinformation has been used to justify slavery and discrimination. The *Richmond Enquirer* of 1851 went to great lengths to prove that "No such thing as a negro government has ever existed in Africa." The paper apparently was ignorant of the accomplishments of the powerful Songhay empire in west Africa (before 1492) and its university at Timbuctu that taught literature, law, and surgery to students from Africa, Europe, and Asia. Senator John C. Calhoun claimed slavery made Africans "so civilized and so improved, not only physically, but morally and intellectually."

These distortions of the Negro's history did not end with slavery nor remain the exclusive property of Southerners. Only recently many Northern textbooks gave this view of the slave:

> As for Sambo, whose wrongs moved the abolitionists to wrath and tears, there is some reason to believe that he suffered less than any other class in the South from its "peculiar institution." The majority of the slaves were adequately fed, well cared for, and apparently happy. . . . Although brought to America by force, the incurably optimistic negro soon became attached to the country, and devoted to his "white folks."

This passage was not written by white Southerners; it appears in the 1940 printing of the widely used college text *The Growth of the American Republic*. The authors are Samuel Eliot Morison and Henry Steele Commager. Distortions of Negro history are still deeply embedded in our history and folklore.

Historians have habitually ignored Negro contributions to most phases of American life, particularly the exploration of the new land and our great post-Civil War industrial growth. Few Americans are aware that Negroes explored the West with Lewis and Clark or Fremont; that a Negro named Matt Henson (with the Peary polar expedition of 1909) was among the first men to stand atop the world; that Negroes contributed a thousand patents to America's industrial thrust just a half-century after Emancipation; that a Negro surgeon performed the first successful operation on the human heart; and that a Negro, Mme. C. J. Walker, was the first American woman to earn a million dollars.

American Negroes have played a hitherto unheralded part in the history of the last Western frontier. The Ninth and Tenth Cavalry, composing a fifth of all the cavalry assigned to pacify the

West, were all-Negro regiments. They patrolled from the Rio Grande to the Canadian border, from St. Louis to the Rockies. Their enemies included Sitting Bull, Geronimo, and Billy the Kid, and their white scouts included Kit Carson, Buffalo Bill, and Wild Bill Hickok. Despite discrimination they earned their share of Medals of Honor and could boast the lowest desertion rate in the Army. Among their proud commanders was John J. Pershing, who won his nickname of "Black Jack" leading a company of the Tenth against Indians and bandits in Montana, against Spaniards in the charge at San Juan Hill, and against Pancho Villa in Mexico.

Americans are unaware of Negro gallantry in defense of the nation during wartime. Fifty-one Negroes have earned the country's highest military decoration, the Medal of Honor. Five thousand Negroes fought for General Washington (largely in integrated units) and American independence, or in the integrated Navy of John Paul Jones. Two battalions of Negroes fought alongside Andrew Jackson at New Orleans to drive off the last foreign invasion of the United States. Others fought in the war for Texas independence, from the defeat at the Alamo to final victory at San Jacinto. More than 200,000 Negroes who fought in the Civil War to save the Union and to end slavery won the praise of their commanders in the field and their Commander-in-Chief in the White House. Negro infantry and cavalrymen helped tame the West, fighting outlaws, Sioux, Comanche, and Apaches. These same units went on to fame and glory in 1898 with Teddy Roosevelt's Rough Riders in the charge at San Juan Hill. In World War I entire Negro units won the French *Croix de Guerre;* in World War II Negroes fought in every theater of the war, and thousands of Negro volunteers helped drive back the Nazi counterattack during the Battle of the Bulge.

This information is not common knowledge largely because it has been obscured by the same mythology of racism that has made us deaf to the Negro's cry for justice. By eliminating the myth and distortion that surround the Negro's past we can search the real background of our present problems and find some of the intellectual tools necessary for solving them. If understanding leads to friendship, then a study of the Negro's part in history can illuminate one path to this goal.

But American Negro history is important for other reasons. It provides a greater truth, a fully dimensional picture of America. Part of our denial of justice to the Negro has been our consistent distortion of his positive role in our society. All Americans can appreciate contributions made to the country under the burdens of slavery or the crippling effects of discrimination. From this American story we can learn anew that the fate of each is bound to the rights of all, and that the price of liberty is still vigilance and struggle.

For Negro students a correct portrayal of the Negro's part in history will serve justice as well as truth. *Amsterdam News* columnist James L. Hicks recalls his days in Central High School, Akron, Ohio:

> I was the only Negro in my history class, and the way my Beard & Beard history book presented the Negro and the way my history teachers taught what little they did teach about the Negro was more than enough to make me cut history classes and almost enough to make me cut out from school altogether.

Such Negro students can learn that their forefathers also had important historical roots deep within the soil of their new homeland.

This book seeks to put the Negro in appropriate places in the American history curriculum, unit by unit of study. Its main categories are those of typical American history courses taught in our secondary schools, not those of "Negro history."*

---

*The central focus of this book is the integration of the Negro into the American history course of study. But it may also be used for related projects. For example, a teacher who wishes to integrate a senior high course on Problems of American Democracy may rely upon those materials which stress segregation and other forms of racial conflict. In instances where the curriculum calls for separate units on the contributions of each of America's minorities, material on the Negro may be culled from the various units presented here. Special courses on the Negro in American history may use materials and even the format of this particular unit-by-unit development.

Its purpose is to offer a framework for the full-scale integration of Negro contributions into the existing American history course of study. For example, Negro cultural figures of the Colonial period should be studied when the class studies cultural attainments in the colonies; Negro inventors of the post-Civil War period when the class studies the contributions of Bell, Edison, and Westinghouse; Negro frontiersmen when the class discusses the frontier.

This book was started during the 1966 Summer Institutes on Integration sponsored by the New York State Education Department at the College of New Rochelle. Institute Director Dr. George Blair, staff members, and participants helped evaluate some of the concepts and methods advanced herein. I particularly wish to thank my Associate Coordinators, Patricia Green and Thomas Harrington, for their help. Miss Green's bibliography of audio-visual aids was most useful.

This book received the aid and encouragement of Mrs. Nida E. Thomas, of the New York State Education Department's Division of Intercultural Relations in Education. Mr. Vernon Alleyne of the Division of Continuing Education worked many hours helping to shape both form and content.

My deep gratitude goes to Sara Jackson, of the National Archives, for her unstinting aid in securing valuable information on many phases of American Negro history from the files of the War Records Office. James C. Evans, of the Office of the Assistant Secretary of Defense, has been most helpful in providing me with significant leads, records, and pictures. Frank Jennings, Education Consultant to the New World Foundation, has made important suggestions as to methods and goals important in the classroom use of these materials. Many thanks are also due Doxey A. Wilkerson, Margaret Schwarz, Erwin A. Salk, Stewart C. Miller, and Diane Horwitz.

I am indebted to Professor John Ether of the State University of New York at Albany for providing me with the lively forum of his Teacher Institute to present my viewpoint and materials to his young teachers. Stan Wexler and Blanche Mayer of the Publications Department of the Anti-Defamation League have also been most helpful to me.

My seven years of teaching at Woodlands High School, Hartsdale, New York, have allowed me to work with one of the brightest and most energetic teaching staffs in the country. I do appreciate their willingness to test materials, to argue points of methodology and concept, and to relay their own and students' reactions. Teachers Dan and Linda Smith particularly have given generously of their time and effort to projects such as this on American Negro history. Kenneth Haskins has been tireless in his criticism and his faith.

WILLIAM LOREN KATZ

September 1967

Preface to the Revised Edition

On the day this book was published, April 6, 1968, two startling events focused nation-wide attention on black history. At White Plains High School, New York, black and white students, demanding more emphasis on the history of Afro-Americans, went on strike and shut down the school. Only a few hours earlier, on the previous evening, Dr. Martin Luther King, Jr., had been assassinated in Memphis.

Much has taken place since that fateful week in 1968. Black history has become, on the one hand, a major demand of student activists throughout the nation and, on the other, a target of abuse for diehard defenders of establishment views. It has not only survived the battle, but now holds a prominent place in many college curriculums. More than a few school systems have integrated black history into their existing American history courses or have added new courses in black studies. Despite the carping and sniping of many critics, black history has become a valid subject for research and discussion, in classrooms and out.

On this second anniversary of the original publication, I find no reason to alter the basic approach here offered secondary school teachers. Black history still needs to be integrated into existing U.S. history courses. Even though many curriculums now include courses in black history and literature, there is always the danger that these will disappear after black militants and their white supporters have stopped exerting pressure. So today's educators must ensure that regular courses in American history continue to include the problems of racism and the contributions of Frederick Douglass, W. E. B. DuBois, Marcus Garvey, and Malcolm X. Such black writers as Langston Hughes and Richard Wright must find a place in regular literature courses—whether separate courses on black literature stand or fall. An amplified evaluation of this issue by several educators, including myself, will be found in the *Journal of Negro Education* for September 1969.

W. L. K.

New York, 1970

Contents

14

Contents

Teachers' Guide to American Negro History

Chapter 1

THE INTEGRATED CURRICULUM AND THE TEACHER

Early in my teaching career I served under a principal whose approach to teaching Negro history was made known only during Negro History Week. Each February he posted a notice that requested his social studies teachers to spend one class period "discussing famous Negro leaders." Obviously, he thought this notice fulfilled the Board of Education directive to observe Negro History Week. It provided the teaching staff with neither information nor guidance—nor any further explanation. Needless to say, the notice was promptly signed (as he required) and universally ignored. We teachers suspected he was well aware of this.

This single-lesson approach had defects, even if carried out to the letter. First, it reduced Negro contributions to the attention of

17

one lesson, itself a mockery of Negro accomplishments. Since it interrupted the course of study in each class, it created situations that could be embarrassing to Negroes and annoying to whites. For the teacher it promised an uncharted sea without a compass. Finally, it segregated the Negro again, honoring him in grand isolation.

The purpose of this book is to give the classroom teacher the basic tools necessary to integrate his American history course. It does not focus on Negro leaders alone, and it makes the teaching of American Negro history a lesson-by-lesson operation. The book offers the teacher significant information, fundamental research materials, audio-visual aids, and some suggestions about basic methodology.

The Teacher and Key Concepts

The teacher is, of course, the key factor in the success of any unit of study. His knowledge of his subject and his students, his sincerity and enthusiasm can insure the success of his labor. This is certainly true about the use of materials on the Negro. If a teacher feels that teaching about the Negro is unnecessary or harmful, or if he simply resents using the word "Negro" in his class, his efforts will meet with little success. At the same time, an educator must realize that more positive attitudes on his part will not win over a hostile class, interest each student, or lower the dropout rate.

Teachers will find, however, that the new materials will interest their classes, regardless of the racial composition. The reasons are not difficult to ascertain: the material is fresh; it is often rife with social conflict; and it is exciting to find hidden dimensions to our nation's history. For these reasons student motivation should be higher than usual.

Teachers will also discover that the introduction of Negro history will often generate a resistance born of years of life in white America. Textbooks and mass media have hitherto conveyed (very effectively, too) a degrading picture of the Negro's past. The student, Negro or white, will not easily abandon his view of Africa as a land of jungles and savages. Teachers who have introduced information about Negro explorers to junior high school classes have been met with shouts of "I don't believe it!" A Negro social studies teacher recently told me that for years he did not believe stories of Negro accomplishments until he read about them in a book by a white historian. Replacing the myths of the past with the truth will *not* be easy. It will be challenging.

In discussing the development of slavery and discrimination in America, teachers should not sensationalize the more brutal aspects of racial conflict. "I stay home when that [white] teacher tells about slavery," a Negro junior high school student confided to a Negro librarian. It is not necessary for an eighth-grade class to learn the worst horrors of the slave trade or the details of slave-breeding in ante-bellum Virginia. Vivid accounts of lynchings do not, as intended, arouse sympathy for the victims but rather bring about revulsion or morbid interest on the part of the student listener. It is important, however, to show that the slave was always open to physical and mental abuse and that lynchings and anti-Negro riots were long a part of American life.

At the same time that a teacher presents the story of the Negro's oppression, he should also tell how the Negro resisted that oppression. No people has ever willingly accepted slavery or second-class citizenship; resistance to tyranny was born with tyranny. During a time of repression people make necessary adjustments and fight back in ways that seem to be most practical. Certainly Negro Americans have demonstrated through the centuries the same stubborn bravery and raw courage that have always been a part of man's fight for freedom and justice.

Teachers should point out that the Negro in America has always had whites who are willing to fight for his rights. Although often few in numbers, these whites have risked their fortunes and lives in this battle, and more than a few have suffered physical and financial loss. Some lost their lives. Still, it is important to note that the majority of whites have shown little concern for the welfare of black Americans until recent times.

The role of Negro leaders should not be overemphasized by those teachers who tend to stress biographical history. If students learn only about outstanding Negroes they will be mystified by the problems of today's black ghettos. For several reasons many

Negroes cannot identify with the affluent or successful among their own people. In studying history we must be careful to see that the success of the few does not blind us to the plight of the many. The heights reached in America today by Robert Weaver or Ralph Bunche indicate a potential yet unrealized. Our heroes should not obscure our common people.

A final problem expressed by teachers concerning the application of Negro materials revolves around the classroom use of the word "Negro." "I feel the designation of someone by race is upsetting to my class," maintained a teacher of her integrated class. This teacher acknowledged that she mentioned that American slaves were Negroes, Columbus was Italian, John Jacob Astor and Carl Schurz were German, Al Smith was Catholic, Samuel Gompers was Jewish, and Jacob Riis was Danish—to note a few. Although our texts frequently fail to mention the national or racial background of many who have contributed to America, this neglect should not continue. Questions of race and racism have played a significant part in American life and have influenced our teaching methods and materials.

In training our students for good citizenship we must emphasize both the negative role racism has played in our history and the contributions made by America's many minorities. Teachers will also note a positive response from their classes, regardless of their ethnic composition. "No one is afraid to mention race, religion, or anything else in class discussions," reported a teacher who had once been hesitant about using words that denoted race or religion. If members of a class rebel at the use of words such as Negro or Catholic or Oriental, then the educator must deal with that problem before many others. But most often this feared resistance to racial or national designations arises in the teacher's mind rather than in the student's.

So much has been written and said about the importance of Negroes' learning their own history that one is left with the impression that American Negro history is appropriate for Negroes alone. Nothing could be further from the truth. White people need to know the part the Negro has played in the development of America and the making of its institutions. Since the Negro's self-image is so much a result of white America's views of him and his capacities, it is basic that whites be exposed to the major historical truths about the Negro in Africa and America. As a matter of fact, the question of who is in greater need of this information is a nice but academic one.

Chapter 2

THE NEW MATERIALS
IN THE CLASSROOM

Our impressions of the outside world—and certainly those of our students—come from the printed word and from audio and visual materials presented to us in schools, on television, or in the movies. For this reason it is of transcendent importance that any effort to integrate school curriculums first concern itself with the most useful of the available aids for teachers and students.

A Basic Teacher Reference Library

Since both the Negro contributions to our history and the available references on the topic are largely unknown, it is essential that a school faculty preparing to integrate curriculums be equipped with key information and the most useful materials before it begins.

The following annotated bibliography consists of basic major works on the topic, for teachers and students, and audio and visual aids.

1. John Hope Franklin, *From Slavery to Freedom* (Knopf, New York, 1967), is the most complete history of the Negro in America. The author, dean of today's Negro historians, presents a thorough, balanced picture of the Negro in Africa and America and traces the Negro's progress from the early states of Africa to the America of the post-World War II period. The volume also includes important pictures and one of the best available bibliographies (annotated and paralleling the chapters of the book). Teachers will find this volume useful for its immense storehouse of information. Recommended for high school students doing research.

2. Langston Hughes and Milton Meltzer, *A Pictorial History of the Negro in America* (Crown, New York, 1968, revised edition), is the best available picture history of the Negro American and an invaluable classroom tool. It uses contemporary sketches, photographs, cartoons, and paintings to illustrate the Negro's struggle for survival and freedom in America. Its picture studies of slavery, abolitionism, the Civil War, Reconstruction, and the current scene are particularly good. The text is interesting and clear. This book should be helpful to both teachers and students at all levels. A teacher may wish to keep a copy at his desk for ready reference or class display.

3. Russell L. Adams, *Great Negroes Past and Present* (Afro-American, Chicago, 1964), is an important collection of short, illustrated biographies of Negro figures in America and the world. Its more than 150 listings are grouped under the following categories: I. Contributions to Early History; II. In Early American History; III. From the Civil War Forward; IV. Science and Industry; V. Business Pioneers; VI. Religion; VII. Leaders and Spokesmen; VIII. Education; IX. Literature; X. The Theatre; XI. Music; XII. The Visual Arts; XIII. Modern America. Each section has an introduction that puts the Negro's contributions in perspective; each biography has a brief bibliographical note. Both teachers and students will find this volume an excellent first step in researching

Negro leaders of yesterday and today. The color drawings are suitable for bulletin board display and may be ordered separately from the publisher.

4. J. A. Rogers, *Africa's Gift to America* (Futoro, New York, 1961, revised edition), is an interesting picture history of the Negro in Africa and America. Its visual material on Africa is generally unavailable elsewhere; its chapter on Negro contributions to the exploration and settlement of Western America is very useful. The author, who did his own research and publishing, is prone to unsupported generalizations and some exaggerations, but the pictures alone make this a useful classroom tool.

5. Talcott Parsons and Kenneth Clark, eds., *The Negro American* (Houghton Mifflin, Boston, 1966, and paperback), is the most complete summary of today's racial crisis. Its thirty articles by authorities in various fields touch on the history and present status of the problems arising from Negro-white relationships in America. This book will be invaluable for those covering the current scene. Basically a college text, it will be difficult reading for most students.

6. William Loren Katz, *Eyewitness: The Negro in American History* (Pitman, New York, 1967, and paperback), consists of text, firsthand accounts, and pictures of the Negro's history in America from African backgrounds to the civil rights movement of today. It is designed to parallel a typical secondary school course in American history and is geared to classroom and research work.

7. The McGraw-Hill (New York) filmstrip series entitled *The History of the American Negro* consists of eight color filmstrips of approximately forty frames each. The color pictures, charts, and subtitle texts are interesting stimulants to class discussion. The eight titles are: 1. *From Africa to America;* 2. *Slavery in the Young American Republic;* 3. *Slavery in "A House Divided";* 4. *The Negro in Civil War and Reconstruction;* 5. *The Negro in the Gilded Age;* 6. *The Negro Faces the 20th Century;* 7. *The Negro Fights for the Four Freedoms;* 8. *The Threshold of Equality.* By previewing the filmstrips, the teacher can plan which

frames he wishes to use in particular lessons. This is the most complete filmstrip set produced on this subject, and in organization, clarity, and exciting content far surpasses most filmstrips of any kind.

8. Rediscovery Films (*New York Times,* New York) has produced a series of classroom films on black history that are good enough to be used in theaters and on television. The first, *The Hurdler,* about the life of Dr. Charles Drew, has already won a prize. *Black Men and Iron Horses,* about Negro contributions to railroading, is suitable for social studies classes concerned with railroads, inventors, or the early union movement. The whole series is a fine example of how movies for schools should be made.

9. *Afro-American History Posters* (Pitman, New York) is an attractive collection of fifteen posters showing how blacks have contributed to important aspects of U.S. history: "American Revolution," "Abolitionism," "Slave Resistance," "Civil War," "Reconstruction," "The Last Frontier," "1930's," "Civil Rights Crisis," and so on. Each large two-color poster covers its topic through blowups of rare photographs and contemporary drawings. *A Gallery of Afro-Americans* (also Pitman) is a set of fifty small two-color posters, each featuring a black American famous in history. The gallery includes a wide variety—all the way from scholars to cowboys.

10. Dorothy Sterling, *Forever Free* (Doubleday, New York, 1963), is a history of the Negro from his African origins until Emancipation Day (1863), with the main focus on the history of slavery and the resistance it generated among Negroes. The author's vivid word pictures make exciting reading for junior high students. The book includes drawings and has been successfully used as a supplementary text in many classrooms. Teachers should be aware that the direct quotes and historical information included (and emphasized by the author) are accurate, the product of careful research.

11. Rayford W. Logan, *The Negro in the United States* (Anvil Books, Princeton, N.J., 1957, paperback), is a concise hundred-page history of the Negro in America, followed by the main legal

documents in the Negro's struggle for freedom and equality. The emphasis is on post-Civil War documents. Recommended for teachers and research.

12. Sterling A. Brown, Arthur P. Davis, and Ulysses Lee, eds., *The Negro Caravan* (Arno Press, New York, 1969), is a thousand-page anthology of pre-World War II American Negro writing, divided into the following categories: I. Short Stories; II. Novels; III. Poetry; IV. Folk Literature; V. Drama; VI. Speeches, Pamphlets, and Letters; VII. Biography; VIII. Essays. The most complete collection of its kind, it should be exceedingly helpful for teachers who wish to use literature as a reflection of historical conditions. The anthology is an invaluable guide for English teachers and for research.

13. Herbert Hill, ed., *Soon, One Morning: New Writing by American Negroes, 1940-1962* (Knopf, New York, 1963), offers the essays, fiction, and poetry of Negroes in the generation after the publication of *The Negro Caravan,* and, subsequently, should be most useful for English and social studies teachers of those students doing research.

14. Rayford W. Logan and Irving S. Cohen, *The American Negro: Old World Background and New World Experience* (Houghton Mifflin, Boston, 1967), is a textbook history of black America that is dull to the core and poorly written in parts, but filled with important factual information.

15. August Meier and Elliott M. Rudwick, *From Plantation to Ghetto* (Hill and Wang, New York, 1966), is an analytical history of American Negroes by two noted scholars in the field. It is most useful to teachers as a guide to the latest findings on the entire subject and may be used by brighter high school students. Its annotated bibliography includes an excellent analysis of the most important current materials.

16. Benjamin Quarles, *The Negro in the Making of America* (Collier, New York, 1964, paperback), is a popular history of the Negro in America. It is organized according to the main chronological periods of our history and combines much valuable information with an adroit writing style. It should be useful for teachers as a general survey of the subject. Chapter 3 on slavery

and Chapter 4 on the non-slave Negro are particularly interesting studies that high school students can consult with profit.

17. Eli Ginzberg and Alfred E. Eichner, *The Troublesome Presence* (Mentor, New York, 1966, paperback), is a scholarly yet readable survey of the Negro in American history. Two-thirds of the book is devoted to the period before 1877. Its arrangement follows the chronology of American history. Recommended for teachers and high school students doing research.

18. Herbert Aptheker, ed., *A Documentary History of the Negro People in the United States* (Citadel, New York, 1969, and paperback), is the most complete documentary history of the Negro American. This massive labor of love covers the period from colonial times to 1910 through the words of the Negroes who helped shape that history. It has received unstinting praise from Negro scholars and has been successfully used in high schools.

19. August Meier and Elliott Rudwick, eds., *The Making of Black America* (Atheneum, New York, 1969), is the best collection of scholarly articles on black history now available. However, since the material introducing these selections is scant, the book is really for teachers rather than students.

20. Joanne Grant, *Black Protest* (Fawcett, New York, 1968, paperback), is a fine collection of articles and documents having to do with black protest. The selections covering the post-1954 period are unequaled anywhere. For teachers the book is a must; for high school students, a useful source of information.

21. Lerone Bennett, Jr., *Before the Mayflower* (Johnson, Chicago, 1962, 1964, and 2d. rev. ed., 1969, Pelican paperback), is a forcefully written history of the Negro in America from 1619 to 1968. Its earliest chapters on Africa and the pre-Civil War periods are exciting and informative, and it includes many interesting pictures. Teachers and high school students should find it valuable for supplementary reading or research.

22. Arna Bontemps, *100 Years of Negro Freedom* (Dodd, Mead, New York, 1967, paperback), is a history of the years following the emancipation of the Negro in America. A useful volume for outside reading in secondary schools, it takes a bio-

graphical approach, focusing on such figures as Booker T. Washington, W. E. B. DuBois, editor T. Thomas Fortune, P. B. S. Pinchback, and A. Philip Randolph. Recommended for supplementary text or as a research tool for secondary schools.

23. The Doubleday-Zenith series (Doubleday, New York, 1965-1967) is an increasingly successful effort to produce an American Negro history series for slow readers. Of its eight current 128-page, illustrated volumes in hard cover and paperback, the ones on the post-Civil War period are excellent. Some of the volumes are biographical, while others are historical-chronological. They introduce students to superb artists as well as some fascinating history.

24. Charles Crowe, ed., *The Age of Civil War and Reconstruction, 1830-1900* (Dorsey, Homewood, Ill., 1966, paperback), is an outstanding collection of essays by leading authorities on nineteenth-century United States history. The scope of this volume is far broader than the title indicates. For students of Negro studies it covers the following topics: 1. Racism's Origin in America; 2-4. The South During Slavery; 5. Abolitionism; 6. Lincoln and Emancipation; 7. Causes and Nature of Civil War; 8 and 9. Reconstruction; 10. Triumph of Racism in the South and North. Each section is introduced by an informative essay that concludes with a valuable bibliography. The selection of essays and essayists provides a broad spectrum of opinion and information.

25. Irvin H. Lee, *Negro Medal of Honor Men* (Dodd, Mead, New York, 1967), is the exciting story of the Negro Medal of Honor recipients and the exploits that earned them this highest U.S. military decoration. Sergeant Lee has uncovered forty-five Negroes who earned this medal and told their stories from long-buried historical records. He includes chapters on the Civil War (III), Indian Wars (V), Spanish-American War (VI), Korea (II), and World War II any beyond (VII). Useful to secondary school students for outside reading or research.

26. Carter G. Woodson and Charles H. Wesley, *The Story of the Negro Retold* (Associated Publishers, Washington, D.C., 1959), and *Negro Makers of History* (Associated Publishers,

Washington, D.C., 1958), are textbook histories of the Negro directed toward secondary school students. The former is written for senior high students, the latter for those in junior high grades. Both are illustrated and useful books, containing much basic information on the many Negro contributors to American history. Recommended as supplementary texts, or as a starting point for student research.

27. Warren J. Halliburton and Mauri E. Pelkonen, eds., *New Worlds of Literature* (Harcourt, Brace & World, New York, 1970), is a book of literature about Negroes and other minorities and is directed toward slower high school readers. The editors, two teachers, have adapted adult material for classroom reading. Negro figures covered include Harriet Tubman, test pilot Eddie Dwight, Marian Anderson, Langston Hughes, Althea Gibson, and Rafer Johnson, plus many others in the fictional pieces. Students are also introduced to the poetry of Langston Hughes, Paul Laurence Dunbar, and others. This fine volume, which would seem to be just what English teachers desirous of integrating their literature courses have wished for, has a superb teachers' guide with page-by-page suggestions for using the book in class. Highly recommended to all secondary school students for both social studies and English classes.

28. John Henrik Clarke, ed., *American Negro Short Stories* (Hill and Wang, New York, 1966, and paperback), is a fine collection of short stories by thirty-one Negro authors from W. E. B. DuBois to James Baldwin. Unfortunately for teachers, the stories are not preceded by introductory material about either the author or the setting, although biographical information about the authors appears in the back and the editor has included an excellent (if too brief) introductory essay. Recommended for high school students in English or social studies classes.

29. Dorothy Sterling, *Tear Down the Walls* (Doubleday, New York, 1969), is a history of the civil rights movement dating back to the days of slavery. Well written and interestingly illustrated, the book is recommended for all students.

30. Gilbert Osofsky, *The Burden of Race* (Harper & Row, New York, 1967), is a fine documentary study of white racism

through the ages, with brief "interpretive" introductions that clarify difficult historical points. Highly valuable for teachers and senior high school students doing research on black history.

31. Philip T. Drotning, *A Guide to Negro History in America* (Doubleday, New York, 1968), is a state-by-state listing of famous landmarks in black history. It would be particularly useful for a program of field trips, since many of the important places are specifically located. In addition, teachers and students can make good use of it as a guide to research..

32. Bradford Chambers, *Chronicles of Black Protest* (Mentor, New York, 1968, paperback), a good brief documentary history of black protest in America, will be helpful for teachers and students.

33. *The American Negro: His History and Literature* (Arno Press, New York, 1968-1970), is a 141-volume series of books that have made black history or recorded it. Selected by an advisory board of one white and eight black authorities, they range from works by scholars to autobiographies by cowboys and soldiers and are indispensable for anyone doing research or outside reading on black America. C. Vann Woodward has called it "the most important response so far to the need for Negro history." Each school and public library should certainly have a set. When ordered for secondary schools the books are accompanied by a comprehensive teachers' guide that details the many uses of each volume in the social studies curriculum.

Specific Teaching Goals

In teaching American Negro history, the teacher may choose to keep these specific goals in mind:

1. To show that the Negro has contributed to the many aspects of American life since his arrival on the continent with the Spanish explorers.

2. To demonstrate that the Negro has made his contribution to America despite slavery and the legalized repressions of the Jim Crow system.

3. To help students of every race in today's America understand the Negro's role and difficulties in American history, and how he has contributed to our culture and institutions.

4. To show that the Negro's part in our history must be seen in the context of the larger picture of American growth and problems.

5. To demonstrate that Negroes never willingly accepted slavery or second-class citizenship but battled in valiant and practical ways to achieve the promise of America.

    a. The civil rights drive began long before the 1960's.

    b. Beginning with the Quakers of Colonial times, important whites, as individuals or in groups, stood ready to help the Negro in his fight for justice and equality.

6. To help students understand that the fight for equal rights is a reform movement aimed at the democratization of American life and the completion of America's promise of freedom to all.

7. To help deepen the students' understanding of the social sciences:

    a. by pointing out the manifold nature of man and his society;

    b. by fostering understanding among people to overcome ethnocentrism;

    c. by using the Negro experience in America as a measuring rod for American growth and limitations during various historical periods.

8. To instill in Negro students a pride in their African and American heritage; to instill in other students an understanding of the Negro's contributions to the nation.

Daily Planning: Some Specific Examples

Once familiar with his subject and sure of his goals, the teacher is prepared to weave the new material on the Negro into the curriculum. It is not necessary to announce to a class that this is to be done, although some teachers have done this, explaining why (citing the textbook omissions and distortions), and have conducted rather lively and interesting lessons around this point itself. Regardless of his initial approach, the teacher will continue to focus on the basic goal of presenting American history, relating the Negro's presence and his contribution to that larger goal.

There is *no special methodology* to be used in teaching about the Negro role in our history. A teacher should use any methods that he has successfully employed in the past—developmental lessons, homework, class discussion, outside reading assignments, committee work, dramatizations, charts, movies, filmstrips, bulletin board displays, research projects, etc. This material should not be highlighted; rather, it should be painlessly made part of the lesson or course of study. This will vary somewhat from teacher to teacher, class to class, grade level to grade level. It should be part of an overall effort to provide credit to all of the American minorities that have been denied their due in our texts or courses.

To illustrate how this may be accomplished, let us take the contributions of Frederick Douglass and see where they may be applied in an American history course. This significant American played an important part in many nineteenth-century American developments—slavery, the Underground Railroad, abolition, women's rights, word reform movements (Irish freedom, temperance, world peace, Corn Law repeal, etc.), as Civil War adviser to President Abraham Lincoln, in early civil rights struggles, as a critic of Reconstruction, and in government service (including the diplomatic service). Of course, he can be discussed *in toto* as an American reformer, with his other contributions presented as background and sidelight. But Frederick Douglass' contributions may also be discussed separately in the following categories, forming segments of lessons long a part of the curriculum.

1. *Slavery.* Douglass was a slave for twenty-one years; his three autobiographical works paint a vivid picture of the slavery he knew. He also describes his escape from bondage.

2. *Abolition.* Douglass was a foremost abolitionist orator and leader, close associate of Garrison, Phillips, and Birney, editor of *North Star,* agent of the Underground Railroad, friend of John Brown, and prolific writer for the anti-slavery cause.

3. *Women's rights.* His speech at the first Women's Rights Convention, Seneca Falls, New York, 1848, was decisive in winning passage of the first resolution to demand women's suffrage. He devoted his life to the fight for equal rights for women.

4. *Worldwide reform movements.* Douglass toured Europe on several occasions speaking for Irish Home Rule, against the Corn Laws, for temperance and world peace.

5. *Minority rights.* Douglass campaigned for equal rights for members of the human family. He championed the cause of public education, abolition of capital punishment, better treatment for the mentally ill and those in prison, justice for the Indian, and fair treatment for Orientals, Jews, and other persecuted groups. He spoke for those civil liberties protected by the First Amendment.

6. *Civil War.* During the war Douglass served as an adviser to President Lincoln, raised troops for the Union Army, and constantly urged the government toward a more democratic policy in the treatment of its Negro troops.

7. *Reconstruction.* During this period and the tragic failure of the plan, Douglass urged the government to protect the freedmen and halt the growing Klan outrages upon Negroes and their defenders in the South.

8. *Civil rights.* Douglass was an early battler for Negro rights. He conducted "freedom rides" and "sit-ins" aboard New England trains, and his philosophy of struggle to eliminate unjust laws was remarkably like the views espoused by today's civil rights leaders.

9. *Caribbean diplomacy.* In *Life and Times of Frederick Douglass,* he describes his several diplomatic missions for the federal government, shedding interesting light on early American Caribbean diplomacy.

Another example can serve to illustrate how the Negro as a causal factor can be placed in a traditional developmental lesson. In discussing "reasons for American acquisition of Florida in 1819," texts note American interest in Florida's fertile land, weak Spanish control of Florida allowing for Indian and pirate depredations, and the American desire to eliminate a foreign nation from the continent and borders of the United States. Another crucial factor, long ignored, was the prevalence in Florida of free and prosperous Negro settlements, composed of men and women who had fled slavery in the United States to find a haven in this Spanish land.

Since Colonial times bondsmen from Georgia and other parts of the South had fled to Florida. Some joined the Seminoles and a few rose to leadership in the tribes. Others gathered in their own colonies along the river banks, establishing homes and plantations. These Florida colonies were a threat to the slaveholding system in America, for they (1) provided a home for runaways, thus encouraging slaves to escape, and (2) exposed the myth that the Negro was suited only to slavery. A crucial factor in United States invasions of Florida and its eventual purchase was the demand of slaveholders that their government seize this haven for slaves. The lesson should include this aspect of our relations with Florida before its purchase.

Since this information on Florida Negroes is new, teachers may expect increased interest from the class. In some classes this lesson has elicited the following questions from students:

1. How did the Seminoles treat the Negroes who joined their tribe? Did Negroes rise to leadership in the tribes?

2. What kind of relationships developed between Indians and Negroes throughout the frontier? Were Indians as prejudiced as whites?

3. Did many Negroes escape to the West? Did any become frontiersmen like Daniel Boone, Davy Crockett, and Jim Bowie?

4. How did the Negroes in Florida live and get along?

The unit on the early westward movement provides some answers to these questions, and the annotated bibliography indicates where other answers can be found.

Committee Work and Dramatization

Outside research has long been a useful way to enrich the curriculum and stimulate independent study. By assigning committee work the teacher will open many new avenues of knowledge to his students.

Let us take a sample committee topic and see how a teacher might make certain that Negro contributions were included in the report of a committee. The topic is "Colonial Figures of Importance"; the teacher asks the committee to identify and discuss those men and women who contributed to American life before the year 1800. The teacher might submit to the committee a list of typical Colonial leaders: Benjamin Franklin, George Washington, John Peter Zenger, Alexander Hamilton, Ann Hutchinson, and Cotton Mather. To this list he need add only the names of Negroes Benjamin Banneker, Phillis Wheatley, and Richard Allen, a scientist, poet, and churchman respectively. If the committee members have difficulty in locating information or books about these three (the teacher can anticipate this through a check of the school and local libraries), he can order books in advance or suggest those that are available.

Let us say this committee has gathered its findings and wishes to present them through a dramatization based on the *Meet the Press* program. Negroes need not be played by Negroes, nor whites by whites. If the committee decides to illustrate the contributions of the Colonial figures they chose, the class will have an opportunity to see charts developed by students, showing efforts of important Negroes as well as whites.

Dramatizations are a powerful way of presenting material on social conflict. Teachers have assigned various committees the topic of slavery, each committee given the viewpoint of a special historical group (slaves, slaveholders, free-soilers, abolitionists, popular sovereignty men). An abundance of material by actual participants has been reprinted in paperback and is easily available. Harvey Wish's *Slavery in the South* (Farrar, Straus, New York, 1964) includes the viewpoints of slaves, owners, and visitors. Once having gathered the material, the groups can agree upon a debate and the class may be invited to offer questions and comments.

Another dramatic way to present committee findings to the class is through the reading of a set of fictionalized letters. For example, a committee reporting on American reformers of the Jacksonian era can develop a set of letters which might have been written by reformers Horace Mann, Dorothea Dix, Frederick Douglass, and Harriet Tubman. The letters might discuss incidents that demonstrate the interest of each reformer, his methods, problems, and successes. Members of the class might wish to write answers to these letters.

Teachers who wish to offer plays by Negro and white playwrights on Negro themes will find many from which to choose.
Martin Duberman's documentary play about American Negro
history, *In White America* (Signet, New York, 1965, paperback),
has been succesfully staged by secondary school students. Lorraine
Hansberry's *A Raisin in the Sun* (Random House, New York,
1959, and paperback) and *The Sign in Sidney Brustein's Window*
(Random House, New York, 1965, and paperback) portray aspects of Negro urban life today. The prolific Langston Hughes's
Five Plays (Indiana University Press, Bloomington, 1963) touch on
various aspects of Negro life and white prejudice. LeRoi Jones's
Two Plays: The Dutchman and The Slave (Morrow, New York,
1964) treat aspects of Negro history. Louis S. Peterson's *Take a
Giant Step* (French, New York, 1954) is a moving play about
prejudice.

In the area of plays on Negroes or prejudice specifically designed for young people, there are several sources. Willis Richard-
son and Mary Miller have edited *Negro History in Thirteen Plays*
(Associated Publishers, Washington, D.C., 1935), a collection
directed more toward elementary than secondary school students.
Truda Weil and Frances H. Kohan have written four plays for
school use, *Men Are Brothers* (Anti-Defamation League, New
York, 1962), which are also directed to elementary school students. Both the Anti-Defamation League and the National Conference of Christians and Jews have available plays that treat the
topics of brotherhood and tolerance for students of various ages.

Use of Original Source Materials

Increasingly, social studies teachers are offering their students
actual source materials—original documents and other writings.
Often these convey emotions as well as facts, making people and
events come alive. They also teach students how to evaluate
sources and how to do research.

The most extensive and best collection is the 141-volume series
The American Negro: His History and Literature (Arno Press
and the *New York Times*), largely written by blacks and includ-

ing new introductions by black and white scholars. Thirty of the volumes have been issued in paperback, and for the entire collection there is a comprehensive teaching manual by Daniel C. Smith, a secondary school teacher who has used these materials for years. The Atheneum reprint series *Studies in American Negro Life* includes about two dozen titles, mostly scholarly works designed for college courses. Each has a lengthy introduction by a scholar in the field. Teachers should find most helpful the two-volume *Making of Black America,* a collection of scholarly articles. Schocken Books has reprinted about a dozen *Source Books in Negro History,* which should be valuable to teachers and secondary school students.

Compilations of documents, dating from Herbert Aptheker's *A Documentary History of the Negro People in the United States* (Citadel, New York, 1952, reprinted 1969), now abound. Most of them, like Aptheker's, are for adult readers and scholars. Among those most useful to high school students are Gilbert Osofsky, *The Burden of Race* (Harper & Row, New York, 1967, and paperback); Milton Meltzer, *In Their Own Words* (Crowell, New York, 1964-1966, three paperback volumes); Richard C. Wade, *The Negro in American Life* (Houghton Mifflin, Boston, 1965, and paperback), and Bradford Chambers, *Chronicles of Black Protest* (Mentor, New York, 1968, paperback). Except for the Osofsky work, each of these draws heavily, if silently, from the Aptheker volumes. William Loren Katz, *Eyewitness: The Negro in American History* (Pitman, New York, 1967, revised 1970), an effort to develop a documentary text through classroom use of source materials, has an 84-page teacher's guide.

For creative and knowledgeable teachers, Educational Design of New York offers in its Black Studies Resources a unique set of 465 source pictures on slides. These include drawings, paintings, and photographs of black Americans as they were pictured in their time—Africans, slaves, protesters, cowboys, inventors, famous leaders, soldiers, and so on. Its variety and flexibility allow even nonreaders to analyze source materials. In the accompanying manual each picture is fully identified and placed in its historical context. All the teacher needs is a slide projector.

An essential part of any course about the current scene are books written by blacks who are and have been making contemporary history: Stokely Carmichael, Dr. Martin Luther King, Jr., Julius Lester, Malcolm X, Eldridge Cleaver, H. Rap Brown, and LeRoi Jones. Each school should subscribe to the *Journal of Negro History* and the *Negro History Bulletin,* publications of the Association for the Study of Negro Life and History. The association has also issued reprints of many fine books on black history.

Outside Reading

Many teachers have moved away from the concept of a single textbook while some have discarded the textbook entirely as a teaching instrument, depending instead on outside readings or several books of varied viewpoints. In this growing movement some teachers, often in conjunction with teachers of English, have made excellent use of novels and short stories to illuminate historical information. Outside readings, including fiction, are an excellent way of introducing Negro contributions to the curriculum.

Since 1954 publishers have issued an increasing number of biographies of famous Negroes of the past and present. Author Shirley Graham has written biographies of explorer Du Sable, scientist Banneker, poet Wheatley, reformer Douglass, educator Washington, and scientist Carver. There are many autobiographies of Negro heroes in sports, entertainment, government service, and civil rights activities. Teachers report that Negro and white students have enjoyed reading these stories of accomplishment. A recent and fascinating addition to the field of collective biographies is co-authored by Philip Durham and Everett L. Jones—*The Story of the Negro Cowboys* (Dodd, Mead, New York, 1965), written on the elementary school level, vividly telling the hidden story of the black cowpunchers who helped tame the West.

In fiction there has also been a growing literature that casts light on American Negro history. High school upperclassmen can enjoy Richard Wright's book of short stories about Southern Negro-white relations during the Great Depression, *Uncle Tom's Children* (Signet, New York, 1942, paperback), or his powerful novel of Chicago ghetto life, *Native Son* (Harper, New York, 1941, and

Signet paperback). Junior high school boys and girls have enjoyed reading Dorothy Sterling's *Mary Jane* (Doubleday, New York, 1957), a moving story about a girl who enters an all-white junior high school in the South after the 1954 Supreme Court decision. The Wright books and the Sterling book are available in paperback.

As most students are attracted more by the specific than the general, by a story rather than a history, novels of nineteenth-century Negro life can have an important effect on their knowledge of history. Harriet Beecher Stowe's *Uncle Tom's Cabin,* though obviously dated in style and inaccurate in some historical detail, has had an impact upon high school readers. It is available in several paperback editions. Margaret Walker's starkly realistic *Jubilee* (Houghton Mifflin, New York, 1966) uses fiction and focuses on a single Negro family to highlight the tragedy of slavery and a betrayed Reconstruction. While some teachers may feel this is strong reading for students, its accuracy and reality cannot be denied. Howard Fast's *Freedom Road* (Crown, New York, 1964), a novel of the Negro during Reconstruction, has been successfully used in many secondary school classrooms and is highly recommended for both junior and senior high students. It is available in many paperback editions.

The teacher and the librarian can play an important part in making sure students are able to find books on the Negro. If the teacher is in the habit of issuing a list of biographies and novels that are appropriate readings for the historical period under study, he should include books about Negro Americans. The school librarian should be certain that she has available a collection of these books for students of each grade level.

From the oral or written book reports required by the teacher, it will soon be possible to determine the amount of reading on Negro topics taking place in a class. "Integrated minds are as vital as integrated schools, at the very least," Whitney Young, Jr., has written. He points out that books can perform the important service of showing Negro and white children what the Negro is like, what his potentialities are.

Audio and Visual Aids

While the number of audio or visual aids available for Negro studies is small, it is an ever-expanding field. Teachers may use a number of documentary movies and Hollywood films to demonstrate various aspects of discrimination: *Home of the Brave,* an arresting film that shows the psychological damage prejudice inflicts on a Negro GI; the *Jackie Robinson Story,* about the baseball career of the Negro who cracked the color bar in the major leagues; or *To Kill a Mockingbird,* an exciting film of prejudice in a Southern town. Each of these is available at reasonable rates from commercial companies. (Brandon Films, Inc., 221 W. 57th St., New York, N.Y. 10019, distributes many of these films throughout the country.)

The movie *Raisin in the Sun* presents a touching and graphic picture of Negro life in Chicago, with a realistic portrayal of the Negro family that has never been matched in films. The American Broadcasting Company's *Walk in My Shoes* is an exciting documentary of Negro reactions to life in white America. Both can be effectively used in current events topics and to stimulate discussion of the problems they raise.

Several television and educational films portray Negro figures of earlier periods of American history. *Frederick Douglass,* one of the famous *Profiles in Courage* presentations shown by the Columbia Broadcasting System, is both meaningful and suspenseful, an excellent classroom tool. *Harriet Tubman and the Underground Railroad* describes the daring escapes planned by the slave woman who rescued three hundred people from bondage. It is particularly appropriate for junior high students, for the emphasis is upon action and the major concepts are clear.

As for posters, filmstrips, and records on Afro-American history, the Pitman Company has created an impressive educational package that relies almost entirely on source materials—documents and pictures—to tell its story. As for source readings, Caedmon Records has produced a fine set of black history autobiographies narrated by Moses Gunn and Eartha Kitt. *Silhouettes in Courage,* produced by a black record company, tells the story of black

Americans through eyewitness accounts of slaves, rebels, path-finders, inventors, militants, cowboys, and soldiers.

The National Education Association has published two significant filmstrips on American Negro history for use in schools. *Legacy of Honor* is a lengthy filmstrip history of the Negro in America. It is accompanied by a recording that supplies the narration. Because it is prepared by educators, it follows the school curriculum in American history more carefully than do other efforts. *Suggestions for Teaching* is directed toward teachers and explains some of the materials and methods available to them. A useful booklet that includes the text accompanies the two filmstrips and recordings.

Several important sources of pictures of Negro leaders, past and present, are now accessible. The Association for the Study of Negro Life and History, in Washington, D.C., offers a large display of pictures in various sizes and prices. Afro-Am Publishers of Chicago also offer a series of sketches and brief biographies of Negro leaders suitable for bulletin board display. Louise Jefferson's pictograph of twentieth-century Negro Americans is excellent for bulletin boards. It is available from Friendship Press in New York City.

Some teachers prefer to create their own bulletin board displays, using the artistic talents of their students. Charts, dioramas, maps, and portraits of people and events under discussion are always useful and creative.

Special Events: Trips and Assembly Programs

There are times when the school assembly program can be a vehicle for furthering the integrated curriculum. Many plays, songs, and movies on the general theme of brotherhood and minority group contributions to America can be presented in the auditorium. Several of the films previously mentioned are examples.

Negro speakers may be asked to address the assembly, but it is not necessary or advisable to ask Negro speakers to speak always on Negro history, civil rights, or related topics. A most effective lesson in intercultural relations took place in a New

York high school that had invited a Negro member of the Peace Corps to discuss her work in Turkey before the school assembly. The speaker was then invited into several world geography classes to expand upon her experiences. Several Negro and white students asked her how Turks treated American Negroes and this evoked lively interest. The powerful impact of this speaker was due to her sensitivity to the students, thorough knowledge of her subject, and her enthusiasm—important qualities to search for in evaluating possible speakers of any race. The Peace Corps veteran then addressed the faculty.

The school auditorium is also an appropriate forum for the presentation of interesting class-originated debates, dramatizations, panel discussions, etc. Administrators of assembly programs and teachers should be aware that activities that are successful in class may not be as well received by the larger audience of a school assembly. Teachers should follow good assembly programs with class discussions, compositions, or further investigation.

Class trips are a normal part of the offerings of many secondary schools. For those who wish to integrate their trip program with the American history course of study, there is an excellent booklet available from the American Oil Company (free of charge), *American Traveler's Guide to Negro History* (American Oil Co., New York). It lists, state by state, the locations of historic landmarks in American Negro history. The booklet includes pictures of many of the sites and some valuable historical information. Teachers and students will also find the booklet crammed with information about Negro contributions to the country's westward movement, a much-neglected area of study.

Students living in or near New York City will find rewarding a visit to the famous Schomburg Collection of the New York Public Library, the largest single collection of Negro materials in America. The library usually has a display of African artifacts, and class tours are accommodated by the library staff, if notified in advance. Books dating back several centuries may be seen and handled. The special picture collection has been used by many scholars. Since the library is in the center of Harlem, the teacher may wish to include a tour of this area in his trip plans.

United States libraries with Negro history book collections are annotated in Appendix B. For a listing of museums of Negro history and other places of interest, see Appendix C.

Evaluation Procedures

Teachers and administrators will want to evaluate the effectiveness of their newly integrated program in American history. There are many ways of gauging student response and teaching effectiveness that need not be delineated here. A useful method is for the teacher to keep records of classroom responses to the new materials. Teachers may wish to record their own original feelings and their later responses.

One of the best ways of testing student response to the new material is through the quizzes teachers use to help determine student grades. To include Negro materials in each part of the curriculum except the tests would raise serious questions in the students' minds about the importance of the materials and the teachers' sincerity. Many students claim they find out what their teachers consider important only when they take tests.

Test questions on the new information should follow the pattern the teacher uses in his regular tests, and the new data should be fully integrated. To use the previous example of the acquisition of Florida, a test question might be: "Describe the role each of the following played in the U.S. acquisition of Florida: Spain, Negro runaways, Seminole Indians, Andrew Jackson."

Chapter 3

MAJOR UNITS
IN
AMERICAN NEGRO HISTORY

Introduction

The units that follow are generally patterned after those used in secondary school American history courses and typical American history textbooks. The information and annotated bibliographies are designed to demonstrate how the Negro's role as either a causal factor or active participant (or both) may be integrated into the regular course of study. These units are a guide to basic information and materials, and are not meant to be complete or exhaustive. The materials chosen were selected on the basis of relevance to the curriculum, usefulness for teachers, readability for students of various levels, and accessibility.

Each unit is composed of the following parts:

1. A listing of the important dates in American Negro history. This is meant to provide teachers with a brief frame of reference based on time concepts. It is not meant to be complete but consists only of the more significant dates.

2. A brief review of the Negro's contribution to the particular unit under study. It is short and highly selective, indicating the scope of that contribution, and serves as a springboard for further study.

3. An annotated bibliography of the available materials for teachers and students at various levels. The bibliography is not intended to be complete or comprehensive but is designed to be helpful to teachers and students seeking further information on the Negro's role in America. A key factor in the selection of these materials has been their availability, with paperback books given special consideration. Each item is recommended for a particular school readership (for example, teachers, high school upperclassmen, junior high students, junior high slower readers), and preference is given to those readings in each volume that relate most clearly to the unit being studied. To facilitate easy reference, specific sections of volumes are often mentioned and approximate reading levels noted. Suggested methodology (for example, outside reading, research by students, etc.) is sometimes indicated when necessary.

Some materials have been omitted because of their unsuitability to the classroom or the particular reading levels to which they are directed. Others are included with appropriate warnings that teachers may wish to follow. And through simple human error, others have been left out.

To meet the growing interest in the African background of the Negroes who came to the New World, I have prepared a brief annotated bibliography on this topic. Just as teachers of American history may provide the cultural backgrounds of the many national groups that constitute our diverse population, so they may wish to use material on the Negro's place of origin and his multi-faceted culture. This material may be used in either Unit I or Unit IV, or wherever the teacher considers it appropriate.

Bibliography of Africa and the Slave Trade

1. John Hope Franklin, *From Slavery to Freedom* (Knopf, New York, 1967). Chapters II, III, and IV include an excellent summary of African history and civilizations since the dawn of time. The great empires and wars that culminated in the disastrous slave trade are carefully drawn. These chapters will be useful for teachers and high school upperclassmen.

2. Basil Davidson, *The Lost Cities of Africa* (Little, Brown, Boston, 1959, and Beacon paperback), is the hidden history of Africa's cultural contributions to the world, unearthed by the outstanding authority in the field. This study of African urban life and cultural attainments points up the distortions of Africa's past and makes fascinating reading. Useful for teachers and high school upperclassmen.

3. W. E. B. DuBois, *Black Folks Then and Now* (Holt, New York, 1939), is a series of essays focused on the African past. The emphasis is largely on African history and development before and during the slave trade. Useful for teachers.

4. Lavinia Dobler and William A. Brown, *Great Rulers of the African Past* (Doubleday, New York, 1965, and paperback), is the story of five great African rulers and their empires. It is written for junior high students and includes color pictures.

5. Roland Oliver and Caroline Oliver, ed., *Africa in the Days of Exploration* (Prentice-Hall, Englewood Cliffs, N.J., 1965, and Spectrum paperback), provides a picture of Africa in the sixteenth and seventeenth centuries, told in the words of eyewitnesses. Teachers and students will find this approach fascinating as well as informative.

6. Daniel P. Mannix and Malcolm Cowley, *Black Cargoes: A History of the Atlantic Slave Trade, 1518-1865* (Viking, New York, 1962, and paperback), is a readable if horrifying picture of the trade that depleted Africa of its strongest sons and daughters for more than three centuries. Useful for teachers and high school students.

7. McGraw-Hill filmstrip, *From Africa to America* (1965), is largely devoted to a study of African culture and the slave trade. Its clear color pictures and text make it valuable for students of all levels.

This African prince of the eighteenth century represents the wealth and advancement of African culture that textbooks have often ignored. While prohibiting European and American slave traders from penetrating the interior of their continent, many African monarchs sold their prisoners to the slave merchants.
Schomburg Collection, N.Y. Public Library

8. J. A. Rogers, *Africa's Gift to America* (J. A. Rogers, New York, 1961), provides sixty pages of large pictures and text that illuminate African life before the slave trade. This book is of value to teachers and students despite its tendencies toward editorialization and exaggeration.

9. August Meier and Elliott M. Rudwick, *From Plantation to Ghetto* (Hill and Wang, New York, 1966). Chapter I summarizes concisely the latest information on the Negro in the Africa of the slave trade era. The authors discuss the question of African survivals among today's American Negroes. Recommended for teachers and high school upperclassmen.

10. Lerone Bennett, Jr., *Before the Mayflower* (Johnson, Chicago, 1962, 1964 and 2d. rev. ed., 1969, Pelican paperback) has a valuable first chapter on the African background, useful for teachers and students. It includes pictures illustrative of African culture.

11. Basil Davidson, *The African Past* (Grosset & Dunlap, New York, 1967, paperback), presents interesting accounts of Africa from antiquity to the present, by travelers and Africans. Davidson's excellent thirty-seven-page introduction, "Africa in History," and his introductions to the documents make this an invaluable source on the continent for high school students doing research. Highly recommended.

12. Basil Davidson, *Africa in History* (Macmillan, New York, 1969), is probably the best one-volume history of Africa in print, carefully researched yet written in a lively style. Davidson traces African history from its earliest kingdoms to the modern period. Highly recommended for teachers and high school students doing research.

13. Fred Burke, *Africa: Selected Readings* (Houghton Mifflin, Boston, 1969), is a documentary textbook on African history that should be a useful research tool for junior and senior high school students.

14. August Meier and Elliott Rudwick, eds., *The Making of Black America* (Atheneum, New York, 1969, and paperback). In Chapter I teachers will find several helpful scholarly articles on Africa.

Exploration and Colonization
of the New World

Dates to Remember

1442 Portuguese bring first African slaves to Europe.

1538 Estevanico, an African with the Spanish explorers, opens Arizona and New Mexico to exploration.

1619 First Negroes are brought to Jamestown as indentured servants.

1688 Pennsylvania Quakers make first group anti-slavery protest.

1741 Slave revolts erupt in New York and South Carolina.

1773 Slave Phillis Wheatley's book of poems is published.

The European search for new routes to India in the fifteenth and sixteenth centuries led to the exploration of parts of Africa and the New World. The Africans brought to Europe by the explorers soon came to the New World with the *conquistadores*. Negroes traveled with Columbus, DeSoto, Cortez, Pizarro, De Vaca, and Marquette and Joliet. The African Estevanico (or Esteban) led Spanish expeditions into New Mexico and Arizona. In 1779 Du Sable, a Negro fur trader, founded the city of Chicago.

In the Portuguese and Spanish colonies, enslavement of the Negro soon replaced Indian bondage. Besides the fact that the African was accustomed to farming, he was thousands of miles from home and easily marked for recapture by his color. The Indian, on the other hand, often died from the white man's diseases or the rigors of the slave system, or else escaped to his tribe or to the woods which he knew better than his pursuers.

In the Catholic Latin American colonies, the Church often intervened to protect the Negro slave from abuse, sanctified slave marriages, and encouraged the formal freeing of slaves. The Church was interested in the soul of the slave and even admitted Negroes to the priesthood. In 1738 Brother Martin De Porres became the first Negro Catholic priest, and the work he began among orphans still continues in Peru.

From the moment of their capture in Africa, Negroes resisted their enslavement. One hundred fifty revolts rocked the ships of the slave trade. Important revolts broke out in various South American countries, the most famous being the Haitian rebellion against French rule led by Toussaint L'Ouverture during the 1790's. This was the only successful land-based slave revolt in human history. For seventy years runaway slaves in the Portuguese colony of Bahaia held off the armies that had come to crush their flourishing walled city.

The first Negroes brought to the English colonies were not slaves but indentured servants who were liberated after years of faithful service. By 1661, however, Virginia made all newly arrived Africans and children born to them slaves forever. From the beginning these slaves were, as George Washington called them, a troublesome kind of property. They fled to the swamps, to the Indians, or to other colonies; some organized slave revolts which kept the whites in a constant state of military preparedness.

It is important to note that slaves comprised 20 per cent of the Colonial population and were used in both Northern and Southern colonies, as skilled laborers and as field hands, in cities and on plantations. More than a few served in the Colonial militia, fishing fleets, New England factories, or homes of the wealthy, North and South. A free Negro population of sixty thousand tried to improve their economic and social standing in a land that held them in contempt because 90 per cent of their brothers and sisters were bondsmen. In North Carolina, Maryland, and New England, free Negroes were enfranchised for many years. Many others petitioned for their equal rights. Some achieved fame or fortune as doctors, caterers, skilled craftsmen, and teachers. Lucy Terry and Phillis Wheatley, who had been granted their freedom after years of

Phillis Wheatley, brought to America from Africa at the age of nine, became a leading Colonial poet. Her work won the praise of Voltaire, John Hancock, Benjamin Franklin, and George Washington. *Schomburg Collection, N.Y. Public Library*

slavery, received wide recognition for their poetic talents. Miss Wheatley's book of verse became the second book published by an American woman and won the praise of Benjamin Franklin and Governor Hutchinson. George Washington invited her to his headquarters in 1776 because he was impressed with her poem about his part in America's fight for freedom.

Although slavery is the most degrading and most exacting form of labor control, Colonial slavery was different from the harsher bondage that arose after the cotton gin made the slave a cog in a vast machine producing cotton for a world market. It was easier for owners to be more humane during the Colonial period, and the freeing of slaves was not an uncommon practice. In New England, particularly, slaves were often educated and instructed in religion. No one sought to justify slavery except on the ground of economic necessity, and the major Colonial figures (Penn, Washington, Paine, Franklin, Henry, etc.) looked toward its eventual abolition.

Bibliography

1. John Hope Franklin, *From Slavery to Freedom* (Knopf, New York, 1967). Chapters IV and VI to IX cover many of the topics to be developed in this unit. Chapter IV and IX detail the Negro's part in the exploration and labor force of colonial Latin America. Chapter VI discusses the Negro in the English Southern colonies, Chapter VII the Middle colonies, and Chapter VIII the New England colonies. The information is highly detailed, factual, and scholarly, and while it will be very useful for teachers, only the most patient upperclassmen will be able to benefit from it.

2. Lorenzo J. Greene, *The Negro in Colonial New England* (Kennikat, Port Washington, N.Y., 1942, and Atheneum paperback), is an excellent study of the New England Negro, slave and free, during the Colonial period. It is particularly useful for information about successful free Negroes in the Puritan colonies. It is recommended for teachers and high school students doing research.

3. Langston Hughes, *Famous Negro Heroes of America* (Dodd, Mead, New York, 1965), has chapters on Esteban, the Negro

explorer who entered Arizona and New Mexico, and Du Sable, the trapper who became Chicago's first non-Indian settler. Recommended for junior high students.

4. Russell L. Adams, *Great Negroes Past and Present* (Afro-American, Chicago, 1963), has short biographies and drawings of many of the famous Negro Colonial figures: Brother Martin De Porres, Du Sable, Toussaint L'Ouverture, Phillis Wheatley. The text is recommended for research by teachers and students.

5. Ralph Korngold, *Citizen Toussaint* (Little, Brown, Boston, 1944, and Beacon paperback), is the biography of the Haitian slave coachman and his men who led the successful slave rebellion against the French forces of Napoleon. An adult biography, it is recommended for senior high students and for research.

6. Shirley Graham, *Jean Baptiste Pointe Du Sable* (Messner, New York, 1953), is the fictionalized biography of the first settler of Chicago. Recommended for junior high students.

7. Arna Bontemps and Jack Conroy, *Anyplace But Here* (Hill and Wang, New York, 1966, and paperback), has an excellent first chapter on Du Sable that should be useful for senior high students or others doing research.

8. Claire Huchet Bishop, *Martin De Porres, Hero* (Houghton Mifflin, Boston, 1954), is a children's illustrated biography of the Peruvian Catholic priest who, in 1962, became the world's first Negro saint. Recommended for junior high students.

9. William Loren Katz, *Eyewitness: The Negro in American History* (Pitman, New York, 1967, and paperback). Chapters I and II present text, documents, and pictures illustrating free Negro and slave contributions to this period of history. Recommended for general reading and research by students.

10. Lavinia Dobler and Edgar A. Toppin, *Pioneers and Patriots* (Doubleday, New York, 1965, and paperback), is the story of six Negro heroes of the Colonial and Revolutionary eras: Phillis Wheatley, Paul Cuffee (merchant), Benjamin Banneker (scientist), Peter Salem (Bunker Hill soldier), Du Sable, and John Chavis (Southern educator). Junior high students should find these biographies useful for general reading and research. The illustrations, particularly, are well done. Some of the figures in

this booklet may be used in the units that follow the Colonial period.

11. Shirley Graham, *The Story of Phillis Wheatley* (Messner, New York, 1949), is the illustrated biography of the slave poet who achieved international fame during the Colonial period. Recommended for junior high students.

12. Elizabeth Yates, *Amos Fortune, Free Man* (Aladdin, New York, 1950), is the prize-winning story of an African prince who was enslaved during Colonial times and finally won his freedom and the liberty of others. Illustrated. Highly recommended for junior high students.

13. Ann Petry, *Tituba of Salem Village* (Crowell, New York, 1964), is the story of a Negro woman whose testimony was important in the Salem witch trials of the 1690's. Recommended for junior high students.

14. Herbert Aptheker, *American Negro Slave Revolts* (Columbia University Press, New York, 1943, and International paperback). Chapter VIII details the long history of Colonial slave rebellions. Teachers and high school students doing research will find this volume most useful for its documentation of Colonial slave resistance.

15. Dorothy Sterling, *Forever Free* (Doubleday, New York, 1963). Pages 45-54 detail the Colonial slave's drive for liberty through stories of escape and revolt. Illustrated. Makes superb use of actual quotations from the time. Recommended for junior high students.

16. Paul Horgan, *Conquistadores in North American History* (Farrar, Straus, New York, 1963), pages 142-160. This is the story of the two expeditions involving Estevanico. It is well written and recommended for junior and senior high readers.

17. Gilbert Osofsky, *The Burden of Race* (Harper & Row, New York, 1967, and paperback). Chapter I, Part 3, reveals Colonial attitudes toward slavery through documents. For teachers and students interested in research.

18. Rayford W. Logan and Irving S. Cohen, *The American Negro* (Houghton Mifflin, Boston, 1967). Chapter II discusses Negro contributions in the New World during the century before

Jamestown. Chapter III describes black Americans during the Colonial period. Recommended for research by junior high school students.

19. Albert P. Blaustein and Robert L. Zangrando, eds., *Civil Rights and the American Negro* (Washington Square Press, New York, 1968). Chapter I has twelve documents on the legal development of Colonial slavery. For teachers and high school students doing research.

20. August Meier and Elliott Rudwick, eds., *The Making of Black America* (Atheneum, New York, 1969). See pages 25-33 for the definitive essay "Negro Companions to the Spanish Explorers." An excellent reference source for teachers.

The Birth and Growth of a New Nation, 1776-1815

Dates to Remember

1770 Crispus Attucks, a runaway slave, is the first to fall in the Boston Massacre.

1776-1781 Five thousand slave and free Negroes serve in the Revolutionary Army and Navy.

1787 The Northwest Ordinance bans slavery in all land north of the Ohio River.

1787 The Constitutional Convention protects slaves as property in three separate sections.

1787 Philadelphia Negroes, forced from a white church, begin their own church.

1814 Two Negro battalions answer Andrew Jackson's call to defend New Orleans against the British.

American Negroes played a significant if neglected part in the American Revolution. They were with the Minutemen at Concord and Lexington, with Washington at Valley Forge and crossing the Delaware. Some served as pilots in the Colonial Navy of John Paul Jones. A few served as spies for the patriots. The Continental Congress also refused to approve a plan that would have armed masses of Southern slaves. But from the Boston Massacre of 1770 until the British surrender at Yorktown in 1781, five thousand Negroes helped their fellow Americans win victory.

The democratic mood created by the Revolution led to a rise in anti-slavery sentiments. Benjamin Franklin in Philadelphia and Alexander Hamilton in New York formed abolitionist societies, and several towns and colonies banned slavery because it conflicted with the prevailing emphasis on freedom.

The fifty-five delegates to the 1787 Constitutional Convention believed that slavery was doomed. They therefore agreed to extend the slave trade for another generation, grant Congress the power to pass laws providing for the return of slave runaways, and grant the slaveholders extra votes for their human property (the "three-fifths compromise"). These compromises were a setback for those opposing slavery.

The most noted Negro of this period was Benjamin Banneker, a Maryland freeman engaged in scientific work. He built a clock, published a popular almanac, and wrote anti-slavery essays. Thomas Jefferson took a particular interest in Banneker, sent his work to French scientists, and recommended his appointment to the commission that laid out the city of Washington, D.C. After President Washington appointed Banneker to the commission, he helped choose the sites for the Capitol, the White House, and other important government buildings. But by the time Banneker died in 1806 he and other Maryland Negroes had been disfranchised.

Richard Allen and Absolom Jones, Negro civic and religious leaders, also contributed to American life during this period. In 1787, while in prayer in a white Philadelphia church, they were pulled to their feet and led from the sanctuary. They went on to form their own African Methodist Episcopal Church. In 1793 they volunteered their services to fight the Philadelphia cholera epidemic and won the praise of Dr. Benjamin Rush for their great efforts. During the War of 1812 they organized and drilled several thousand Negroes to protect Philadelphia from British attack.

Negroes also played a significant role throughout the War of 1812, on land as well as at sea. An estimated one-sixth of the American Navy was Negro, and others fought on privateers. The famous Leopard-Chesapeake incident, in which the British fired on, halted, and boarded an American ship, involved the seizure of four seamen, three of whom were Negroes. (The three later won their release by proving they were Americans.) Captain Oliver

Perry, who first resented using Negro seamen, praised their gallantry after his famous victory on Lake Erie.

It was during the 1815 battle at New Orleans that Negro land forces distinguished themselves and won the praise of their commander, General Andrew Jackson. Two battalions served under the rugged frontier fighter after he promised them equality of treatment and pay. They fought alongside Choctaw Indians, pirates, Mississippi riflemen, New Orleans businessmen, and Tennessee mountaineers, as well as regular soldiers. This truly American volunteer army decisively defeated the last foreign invasion of the American mainland. General Jackson, in a letter to Napoleon, credited a Negro marksman with shooting British General Packenham.

Bibliography

1. John Hope Franklin, *From Slavery to Freedom* (Knopf, New York, 1967). Chapter X is a summary of the Negro role in the Revolution and the part slavery played in both the Revolutionary philosophy and the thinking behind the Constitution. Recommended to teachers and high school upperclassmen doing research.

2. Benjamin Quarles, *The Negro in the American Revolution* (University of North Carolina Press, Chapel Hill, 1961, and paperback), is a complete and documented study of the Negro's role in the Revolution by one of America's foremost Negro historians. Recommended for research by teachers and high school upperclassmen.

3. William Loren Katz, *Eyewitness: The Negro in American History* (Pitman, New York, 1967, and paperback). Chapter III describes black contributions to the Revolution, the Critical Period, and the War of 1812. Recommended for supplementary reading or research by students.

4. Lavinia Dobler and Edgar A. Toppin, *Pioneers and Patriots* (Doubleday, New York, 1965, and paperback), includes interesting chapters on Peter Salem, hero of Bunker Hill, and Benjamin Banneker's scientific contributions to America. Text and pictures are excellent for junior high school readers.

This Boston monument was erected to commemorate Crispus Attucks and the other four Americans who died in the Boston Massacre. Attucks was a runaway slave who had become a seaman.
Schomburg Collection, N.Y. Public Library

5. The McGraw-Hill filmstrip, *Slavery in the Young American Republic,* is an excellent classroom tool for introducing this unit or summarizing it, for it details the Negro's role in the Revolution, the creation of the Constitution, and the War of 1812. The color pictures are tastefully done, the captions meaningful.

6. Shirley Graham, *Your Most Humble Servant* (Messner, New York, 1949), is the facinating story of Benjamin Banneker, inventor, surveyor, writer, and anti-slavery advocate. A useful appendix includes Banneker's letter to Jefferson and a full recounting of the book's sources. This story should have appeal for junior high and many senior high students.

7. Langston Hughes, *Famous Negro Heroes of America* (Dodd, Mead, New York, 1958), pages 22-30. This is the story of Crispus Attucks, the runaway slave who led the American mob at the Boston Massacre. It is written for junior high students.

8. Mimi Cooper Levy, *Whaleboat Warriors* (Viking, New York, 1963), is a novel of anti-British guerrilla warfare by Negro and white Yankees during the Revolution. It is an exciting and welltold story for junior high students.

9. Dorothy Sterling, *Forever Free* (Doubleday, New York, 1963), pages 63-89. The story of the Negro's role in the American Revolution and the formation of the Constitution. It is an excellent account of these events for junior high readers.

10. The NAACP booklet, *Black Heroes of the American Revolution* (NAACP, 20 W. 40th St., New York, N.Y.), details the role played in the Revolution by twenty American Negroes. It is recommended for research by students and teachers.

11. Langston Hughes and Milton Meltzer, *A Pictorial History of the Negro in America* (Crown, New York, 1968, revised edition), pages 54-65. This book presents pictures and text on the Negro in the American Revolution and the War of 1812, and Richard Allen's formation of the African Methodist Episcopal Church. Recommended for all students and teachers.

12. Dwight Lowell Dumond, *Antislavery* (University of Michigan Press, Ann Arbor, 1961, and paperback), is a well-written, scholarly study of the abolitionist movement. Chapters III and IV discuss the major concepts regarding slavery which grew out

of the Revolution and the making of the Constitution. The analysis of the Constitution presented by Dr. Dumond is of basic importance to teachers who wish to understand why slavery was three times protected in our national document. Recommended for teachers and high school upperclassmen doing research.

13. Lerone Bennett, Jr., *Before the Mayflower* (Johnson, Chicago, 1962, 1964, and 2d rev. ed., 1969, Pelican paperback). Chapter III vividly depicts black contributions to the American Revolution. Teachers and students will find the book useful for research.

14. Leslie H. Fishel, Jr., and Benjamin Quarles, eds., *The Negro American* (Scott, Foresman, Glenview, Ill., 1967). Chapter II has a fine collection of documents on the part black Americans played in the American Revolution. Recommended for teachers and for high school students working on research.

The Westward Movement

Dates to Remember

1790 America's first treaty (with the Creek Indians) contains a provision requiring the return of slave runaways.

1816 U.S. troops are ordered into Florida to destroy a Negro fort.

1841 William Leidesdorff, destined to become a wealthy and noted Californian, arrives in Spanish California.

1844 George W. Bush leads white settlers into the Oregon territory.

1850 James Beckwourth, a runaway slave who became a famous Indian fighter, discovers an important pass in the Sierra Nevadas.

The westward movement involved Americans of every race, creed, and color. Negroes accompanied the Lewis and Clark expedition, served in the early fur companies that drove into the American wilderness, and accompanied Fremont's three expeditions to the Northwest. Many moved west as slaves, some as slave runaways, but others traveled as free men. But however they came, Negroes were part of the California Gold Rush, the Mormon migration to Salt Lake City, and the exploration of the new land from the Florida swamps to the Rockies and beyond.

Negroes often were able to establish a different relationship with the Indians than that of the whites. The Indians quickly saw that they and the Negroes had the white men as enemies, so black and red men often made common cause. Fur trappers found that Indians trusted their Negro guides and interpreters. Several Negroes were highly successful at converting Indians to Christianity. More than a few Negroes entered Indian tribes, and some rose to positions of leadership. James Beckwourth, to name the most prominent, became chief of the Crow Indians and led them on many raids against their Blackfoot foes. One legend maintains that Beckwourth was poisoned by his tribe when he refused to continue leading them. The Crows buried Beckwourth in their ancestral graveyard so he would always be with them.

The most significant Indian-Negro alliance took place in Spanish Florida where hundreds (perhaps thousands) of runaways from the deep South joined the Seminoles or formed their own free communities. By the end of the War of 1812 Negro families had built homes and plantations in Florida and tended large herds of horses and cattle. Angry slaveholders demanded that the government invade this land, retake their slave property, and punish their Indian allies. Three Seminole Wars resulted, and in all three a basic issue was the freedom of the Florida Negroes. The last of these wars lasted eight years and was the most costly Indian war America ever fought. It resulted in the removal of many Indians and Negroes from Florida to Oklahoma.

Negroes played a significant role in the development of both Texas and California. Negro cowhands tied and branded cattle long before they won their own freedom. From the Alamo defeat to victory at San Jacinto, Negroes, slave and free, fought for Texan independence against Mexican dictator Santa Anna. But the Lone Star Republic quickly disfranchised its free Negroes and demanded their removal from the country.

In California's Gold Rush, slaveholders brought their human property to help in the mining of gold, and more than a few slaves won their liberty by striking it rich for their masters. By 1852 California had the wealthiest Negro community in the United States. Besides Negro gold-seekers, there were Negro teachers, Pony Express riders, and government officials. California Negroes held conventions and petition drives to demand the equal right to testify in court against whites, to vote, and to hold office.

In addition to the active role Negroes played as participants in the westward movement, they became a vital issue in pre-Civil War America. The West became the first battleground in the

struggle over slavery. Slaveholders and free-soilers battled for
control of the Western states, and warfare erupted in Illinois in
1820 and Kansas in the 1850's. White abolitionist Elijah Lovejoy,
a printer, was killed in Illinois, and an Indiana mob broke Negro
abolitionist Frederick Douglass' arm. John Brown used Kansas
as a base to launch raids to liberate Missouri slaves. By 1859 the
Kansas stations of the Underground Railroad were jammed with
slave runaways being sent on to Canada.

The hatred most Westerners felt for slavery was unfortunately
matched by their feeling against free Negroes, whom they often
associated with slavery. In no frontier state could Negroes vote
or hold office; many state constitutions forbade Negroes from even
entering. The flower of democracy that flourished in Western soil
was lily-white.

Bibliography

1. J. A. Rogers, *Africa's Gift to America* (J. A. Rogers, New
York, 1961), pages 82-91. Text and pictures illustrate Negro explorers in the Western lands. Despite a tendency toward exaggeration, this section is a revelation to those who assume that all
pioneers were white. Recommended for teachers and students of all
levels.

2. William Loren Katz, *Eyewitness: The Negro in American
History* (Pitman, New York, 1967, and paperback). Chapter
IV presents the Negro's role in the Western movement from the
Lewis and Clark Expedition in 1804 to the California Gold Rush
of 1849, with pictures of Negro trail blazers, missionaries, trap-
pers, and cowboys, and eyewitness accounts of their exploits.
Recommended for teachers and students.

3. Arna Bontemps and Jack Conroy, *Anyplace But Here* (Hill
and Wang, New York, 1966, and paperback), tells of several
important Negro pathfinders: Du Sable (Chapter I), Beckwourth
(Chapter II), and the Bush family and others (Chapter XVI).
Recommended for high school students and teachers.

4. Dorothy Sterling, *Forever Free* (Doubleday, New York,
1963), pages 55-62, tells the exciting story of the Negroes of
Florida and their Seminole allies. Recommended for junior high
readers.

James Beckwourth, founder of Beckwourth Pass in 1850, was a run-away slave. He served as a scout for General Kearney in California's war for independence, and for many years was chief of the Crow Indians.
New York Public Library

5. Irwin N. Peithman, *The Unconquered Seminole Indians* (Great Outdoors, St. Petersburg, Fla., 1957, paperback), is the story of the Seminole Indians and the Negroes they befriended through three wars with the United States. It is illustrated and useful for junior high students.

6. Langston Hughes, *Famous Negro Heroes of America* (Dodd, Mead, New York, 1954), includes the story of James Beckwourth. Recommended for junior high students.

7. The American Oil Company's *American Traveler's Guide to Negro History* contains much valuable information about Negro participation in the exploration of the West. It is organized according to states and includes excellent photographs and sketches of key people and places. Its emphasis is upon historic landmarks that can be visited.

8. Eugene H. Berwanger, *The Frontier Against Slavery* (University of Illinois Press, Urbana, 1967), is a carefully researched study of anti-Negro prejudice in the Western states and territories and an invaluable guide to research on this topic. Anti-slavery sentiments in the West, it reveals, stemmed from prejudices against black people. The chapters are arranged by territorial sections: Chapters 1 and 2 cover the Old Northwest; Chapter 3, California; Chapter 4, the Pacific Northwest; and Chapter 5, the Middle West. Chapter 6 discusses Western politicians and the slavery controversy.

9. Emma Lou Thorbrough, *The Negro in Indiana* (Historical Bureau, Indianapolis, 1957). Chapters 1-6 cover Negroes who as slaves and free men and women were among the early settlers of Indiana. A useful research tool for studying a particular Negro Western community. Recommended for teachers and senior high students.

10. Russell L. Adams, *Great Negroes Past and Present* (Afro-American, Chicago, 1964), includes sketches and biographical information about William Leidesdorff of California and Edmonia Lewis (sculptress of Negro-Indian parentage). Recommended for teachers and students.

11. Harold W. Felton, *Jim Beckwourth, Negro Mountain Man* (Dodd, Mead, New York, 1966), is the story of the Negro who

became chief of the Crow Indians. Taken from his own 1856 autobiography, it is directed to junior high or younger readers.

12. Merton I. Dillon, *Benjamin Lundy and the Struggle for Negro Freedom* (University of Illinois Press, Urbana, 1966), is a careful study of an early white abolitionist. Its particular focus is on the Western anti-slavery campaigns and abolitionist reactions to the growing slaveholder influence in Texas that finally led to war with Mexico. Recommended for high school upperclassmen and teachers, and useful for research.

13. Ramón Eduardo Ruiz, ed., *The Mexican War: Was It Manifest Destiny?* (Holt, Rinehart & Winston, New York, 1963, paperback), is a series of historical readings on the origin of the war with Mexico and its place in Western history. Since this conflict is so closely related to the questions of slavery and abolitionism, many of the readings touch on these topics. Recommended for high school students doing research on this topic.

14. Henrietta Buckmaster, *The Seminole Wars* (Collier, New York, 1966), is the story of the U.S. government's long battle to subdue the Negroes and Seminoles of Florida. This excellent book is directed toward secondary school students and is the most complete version of this part of American history ever recorded for students. The author has skillfully mixed rare historical material with a compelling writing style. Recommended for research, outside reading, or as a supplementary text for any study of the American pacification of Florida.

15. Harold W. Felton, *Edward Rose, Negro Trailblazer* (Dodd, Mead, New York, 1967), is the story of the early nineteenth-century Negro frontiersman. It is illustrated and is directed toward junior high readers.

16. T. D. Bonner, *The Life and Adventures of James P. Beckwourth* (Arno Press, New York, 1969), is a reprint of the "autobiography" of the famous black frontiersman. A new introduction evaluates the treatment traditionally given black Westerners and Beckwourth by historians.

The South During Slavery

Dates to Remember

1793 Eli Whitney invents the cotton gin.

1800 Massive slave revolt led by Gabriel Prosser is smashed in Virginia.

1822 Denmark Vesey's conspiracy to capture Charleston is crushed in South Carolina.

1831 Nat Turner's Virginia revolt is ended by state and federal troops.

1846 Free Negro Norbert Rillieux devises a vacuum pan that revolutionizes the world sugar refining industry.

By the time of the Civil War, the South's fifteen slave states were the home of eight million whites (of whom 300,000 were slaveholders) and four million Negroes (of whom 250,000 were free). Most of the whites were poor, most of the slaveholders held only a few slaves, and most of the slaves worked on large plantations in the deep South. But through the power of the slaveholder, especially the three thousand holders of fifty or more slaves, the South had become a backward agricultural region devoid of industry, literature, and democracy. The slaveholders made the law and selected congressmen, teachers, ministers, editors, and sheriffs. To justify themselves, to divide the poor whites from the Negroes and to control their slaves, the slavocracy promulgated the theory of white supremacy and made it the *sine qua non* of Southern life.

Negro slaves did much of the work of the South. Most labored in the fields of rice, cotton, and tobacco. But others served in the mansions of the wealthy or became skilled mechanics on plantations or in the cities. On the plantations Negroes lived under rules and laws enforced by masters and overseers; they had no rights any white person was bound to respect. Their diet was poor, their living conditions primitive, and their working hours long. In the cities slaves were controlled less strictly, often made their own contracts, and sometimes worked overtime for pay. They labored on railroads, barges, and construction projects; built ships, hotels, and statues; worked in factories, homes, and laboratories. Several were inventors, and one worked in the laboratory of the U.S. Naval Academy at Annapolis. When white laborers struck for higher pay, slaves were often brought in to replace them.

In the cities the slaves came in contact with the South's free Negro population. Segregated from Southern society, discriminated against at every turn, the free Negroes sought to raise their living standards and offer aid and comfort to their brothers in bondage. Their homes were often the "stations" of the Southern branch of the Underground Railroad, and they forged the passes for the slave runaways. Almost four thousand free Negroes owned slaves, usually relatives they were allowed to buy but not liberate. In New Orleans free Negroes were prominent among the artisans and shopkeepers and contributed a book of French verses to the city's cultural development. Norbert Rillieux, educated in Paris, was writing scientific papers and teaching engineering at twenty-four. His invention of a vacuum pan revolutionized the sugar refining industry of the world. But he chose to live out his life in Paris rather than face the restrictions of his native New Orleans.

The white South used virtually every method to control its slaves. Negroes were forbidden by a Slave Code to hold meetings, learn to read and write, own weapons, or defend themselves. Nightly slave patrols with savage dogs traversed the countryside to prevent escapes and conspiracies. Yet, despite all efforts, slaves escaped, broke tools, ruined crops, murdered masters and overseers, and plotted hundreds of revolts. No revolt could succeed, however, for local, state, and federal militias stood ready to crush all efforts for freedom.

"Slavery," wrote Southern poor white Hinton Helper, "kills everything it touches." Southern legislatures voted funds for slave patrols and slave jails but rarely for schools and libraries. The

Southern poor white faced a life of illiteracy, competition with slave labor, and grinding poverty. Since he accepted the myth that called him superior because of his white skin, he resented the slave rather than the owner, hunted runaways for rewards, and joined the slave patrols. Many poor whites left the South seeking opportunities in the North or West; those who remained were brutalized by America's slave system.

The South during slavery was in a constant state of change. The cotton gin brought vast changes to Southern life, both Negro and white. It turned the South into an aggressive business machine that wore out land and people in a drive for quick profits in an uncertain world market. Both the cotton gin and the planter needs it stimulated were important factors in our Western expansion.

Bibliography

1. Kenneth M. Stampp, *The Peculiar Institution* (Knopf, New York, 1956, and Vintage paperback), is the most scholarly and readable history of slavery available. Chapter I includes an important discussion of why Africans were utilized for Southern labor; Chapters III and IV detail the slaves' resistance to bondage and the harsh methods used to control them. For teachers and high school students who wish to study Southern slavery thoroughly, this is the most important single source.

2. Herbert Aptheker, ed., *A Documentary History of the Negro People in the United States,* Vol. I (Citadel, New York, 1951, and paperback), has documents on every aspect of Negro slave life and resistance. As most documents are presented in their entirety, this volume will be of value mainly to teachers and high school upperclassmen.

3. Milton Meltzer, *In Their Own Words,* Vol. I (Crowell, New York, 1964, and paperback), has many of the Aptheker documents, but in versions edited for use by students. The author's stress in this volume is often on the more brutal aspects of Southern slave life. Useful for teachers and high school students.

4. Eric L. McKitrick, ed., *Slavery Defended: The Views of the Old South* (Prentice-Hall, Englewood, N.J., 1963, paperback), presents the actual arguments long used to defend slavery. An

Nat Turner, whose 1831 slave revolt led to the death of sixty whites, surrenders to authorities. Although slave resistance was rarely this violent, it was omnipresent in Southern ante-bellum life.
Schomburg Collection, N.Y. Public Library

excellent collection of documents for teachers and high school upperclassmen.

5. Harvey Wish, ed., *Slavery in the South* (Farrar, Straus, New York, 1964, and paperback), is the story of slavery told by contemporary slaveholders, slaves, and visitors to the South of the nineteenth century. Excellent for study of plantation slavery. Recommended for teachers and high school students as a classroom supplement or for research.

6. John Hope Franklin, *From Slavery to Freedom* (Knopf, New York, 1967). Chapters XIII and XIV discuss slavery and free Negroes thoroughly, presenting much neglected information on the contributions of free Negroes. Useful for teachers and high school upperclassmen doing research.

7. Ulrich B. Phillips, *American Negro Slavery* (Louisiana State University Press, Baton Rouge, 1966, paperback), is a reprint of the famous apology for Southern slavery first published in 1918. Despite a racist orientation, its thorough documentation makes it useful for those able to separate propaganda from history. Recommended for teachers and high school upperclassmen.

8. Herbert Aptheker, *American Negro Slave Revolts* (International, New York, 1963, paperback), is a thorough examination of Negro resistance to bondage, North and South, from the Colonial period until the Civil War, by the acknowledged authority in this field. Excellent for research by teachers or high school upperclassmen.

9. Dorothy Sterling, *Forever Free* (Doubleday, New York, 1963), pages 91-131. This is the well-told story of slavery and its Southern apologists, and the resistance it generated. For junior high students.

10. Frederick Douglass, *Narrative of the Life of Frederick Douglass* (Dolphin Books, New York, 1963, paperback), is the reprint of Frederick Douglass' 1845 story of his slave life. It is the most important and penetrating of the slave narratives. Recommended for outside reading by high school students.

11. Josiah Henson, *Father Henson's Story of His Own Life* (Corinth, New York, 1962, paperback), is a reprint of the famous well-told slave narrative written by the man who inspired *Uncle*

Tom's Cabin. Unlike Uncle Tom, Henson fought slavery at each step and became a conductor for the Underground Railroad. This book should be useful to teachers and students at all levels.

12. Ann Petry, *Harriet Tubman* (Crowell, New York, 1955), tells of the fearless slave woman who rescued three hundred others from bondage and then led Union attacks during the Civil War. An excellent and readable story for junior high students.

13. Henrietta Buckmaster, *Flight to Freedom* (Crowell, New York, 1958), is the exciting account of the Underground Railroad that spirited slaves out of the South. It is directed toward junior high readers. The same author's *Let My People Go* (Harper & Row, New York, 1940, and Beacon paperback) covers the subject on a higher reading level. Although it has many quotes and few sources are noted, it maintains reader interest and should be useful to teachers and students.

14. *Five Slave Narratives* (Arno Press, New York, 1968), reprints the autobiographies of Lunsford Lane, J. W. C. Pennington, William Wells Brown, Jacob Stroyer, and Moses Grandy. These eyewitness stories, together with the introduction, cast new light on slavery, its profiteers and its victims. Recommended as outside reading for teachers and high school students.

15. The McGraw-Hill filmstrip *Slavery in a House Divided* (New York, 1965) is a useful color filmstrip for students. Its color drawings are realistic and interesting, and important factual information is intelligently presented.

16. Langston Hughes and Milton Meltzer, *A Pictorial History of the Negro in America* (Crown, New York, 1963). Pages 14-41 include valuable text and excellent pictures of free Negroes and slave resistance. Other aspects of these topics are scattered throughout the book, again with clear text and superb pictures. Recommended for all students.

17. Russell L. Adams, *Great Negroes Past and Present* (Afro-American, Chicago, 1963), has biographies and pictures of Joseph Cinque (shipboard slave revolt leader), Denmark Vesey and Nat Turner (slave revolt leaders), Harriet Tubman and Frederick Douglass (slave runaways), and inventors Norbert Rillieux and Benjamin Banneker. Useful for research.

18. Margaret Walker, *Jubilee* (Houghton Mifflin, Boston, 1966, and paperback), is the prize-winning story of the author's great-grandmother, a slave who, later freed, lived during the turbulent years of slavery, Civil War, and Reconstruction. Recommended for high school students.

19. B. A. Botkin, ed., *Lay My Burden Down* (University of Chicago Press, Chicago, 1945, and paperback), is a history of the Negro during slavery, Civil War, and Reconstruction, told in the words of elderly Negroes who survived these times. Told to the Federal Writers' Project of the New Deal, it is useful for high school students doing research, although its organization leaves much to the student.

20. Stanley M. Elkins, *Slavery* (Grosset & Dunlap, New York, 1963, paperback), is a series of essays on aspects of slavery and abolitionism that has received high praise and severe criticism. Particularly useful to teachers is Chapter II, which compares slavery in capitalist America with that in feudal societies.

21. Philip Sterling and Rayford Logan, *Four Took Freedom* (Doubleday, New York, 1967, and paperback), is the story of four great Negro leaders who began as slaves: Harriet Tubman, Frederick Douglass, Robert Smalls, and Blanche K. Bruce. It is exciting reading for junior high students and includes superb illustrations by Charles White. Teachers may wish to assign some of these readings to other parts of the curriculum: Bruce and Smalls could also be used in the part on Reconstruction; Tubman and Douglass in the section on reform and abolitionism.

22. John Hope Franklin, *The Militant South* (Beacon, Boston, 1964, paperback), is a fascinating study of the militaristic and expansionist thinking of the slave South before the Civil War. Useful for teachers and high school students doing research.

23. Sarah Bradford, *Harriet Tubman, The Moses of Her People* (Corinth, New York, 1961, paperback), is a reprint of an 1886 biography of the Negro heroine of the Underground Railroad, written by a white friend. Although the author is by no means a skilled biographer, this is an interesting book that re-creates some of the flavor of the time and does provide a surprisingly large number of valuable documents relating to Tubman's

life. Useful for outside reading or research by junior or senior high students.

24. William Loren Katz, *Eyewitness: The Negro in American History* (Pitman, New York, 1967, and paperback). Chapter 5 describes the many facets of Negro life in the South during slavery in a series of unusual pictures and revealing accounts by slaves, masters, and visitors. Particularly useful for its portrayal of free Negro accomplishments and slave resistance.

25. Thomas Wentworth Higginson, *Black Rebellion* (Arno Press, New York, 1968), is a reprint of five articles, first published in the 1860's, on New World slave rebellions. Useful for research by teachers and high school students.

26. Theodore Dwight Weld, *American Slavery as It Is* (Arno Press, New York, 1968), another reprint, is the best abolitionist pamphlet attack on slavery, proving its inherent evils through the use of documents. Recommended for teachers and high school students doing research on this topic.

27. Bernard Katz, ed., *The Social Implications of Early Negro Music in the United States* (Arno Press, New York, 1969), reprints the earliest important articles on slaves' music. Recommended for research by both teachers and students.

28. Frederick Douglass, *My Bondage and My Freedom* (Arno Press, New York, 1968), is a reprint of Douglass' best autobiography. For teachers or students as outside reading.

29. *Slavery and Slave Resistance* (Arno Press–New York Times) is a hard-hitting color film (26 minutes) stressing the conditions of slavery and the resistance of black people to their bondage. Excellent for class motivation.

30. Julius Lester, *To Be a Slave* (Dell, New York, 1970, paperback), is an original and fascinating collection of slave comments on bondage, held together by forceful editorial comments. Highly recommended.

The Development of the Free North

Dates to Remember

Dates to Remember

1815 Paul Cuffee, a wealthy Negro merchant, helps a group of Negroes reach Africa.

1827 *Freedom's Journal,* America's first Negro newspaper, appears in New York City.

1837 William Whipper, a wealthy Negro and civil rights advocate, calls for non-violent resistance to unjust laws.

1848 Lewis Temple of Massachusetts invents the toggle-harpoon so important to the New England whaling industry.

1855 John M. Langston of Ohio becomes the first Negro elected to political office in America.

Northern Negroes (numbering a quarter of a million by the Civil War) took part in their section's industrial and cultural growth. By the 1830's every Northern state had eliminated slavery, and Negroes, while facing segregation and many forms of discrimination, contributed to the North's commercial expansion. Paul Cuffee of Massachusetts became a shipowner and landowner of great wealth; the year before the American Colonization Society was formed to promulgate the idea, Cuffee led Negroes to Africa, largely at his own expense. James Forten of Philadelphia invented a device for controlling sails that made him a wealthy man. His factory of fifty white and Negro laborers manufactured his device for a growing market. William Whipper, owner of a large Pennsylvania lumberyard, lectured to Negro reading societies, contributed to the Underground Railroad, and developed a theory of non-violent resistance to unjust laws that predated Henry David Thoreau's *Essay on Civil Disobedience* by twelve years. Lewis

Temple, a New Bedford mechanic, invented the toggle-harpoon that has been called the most important single invention in the whaling industry.

Several Northern Negroes contributed to the growing interest in American culture. William Wells Brown, who escaped from slavery, became in 1853 America's first Negro novelist and in 1858 America's first Negro playwright. A world traveler and lecturer, Brown wrote three books on his travels as well as histories of the Negro in America. Frances Ellen Watkins Harper, the most popular Negro poet of the ante-bellum period, published a novel in 1867. Earlier in their careers both Mrs. Harper and Brown had served on the Underground Railroad. Although acclaimed from Dublin to Moscow, Ira Aldridge, who was world famous as a Shakespearean actor, was not permitted to perform in a mixed cast in Baltimore, Maryland.

James W. C. Pennington, a slave blacksmith who escaped to the North, illustrates the role Negro intellectuals played in the fight for Northern civil rights. Pennington learned to read and write, then mastered German, French, Latin, and Greek and won a Doctor of Divinity degree at Heidelberg. He returned to New York, where he led his congregation in several non-violent campaigns against streetcar segregation. In 1841 he published the first text history of the Negro.

Others were part of the pre-Civil War civil rights struggles. Aboard segregated New England trains, Frederick Douglass staged Freedom Rides that led to the abandonment of Jim Crow cars in Massachusetts. Many early Negro protests centered on school segregation, and the first desegregation suit was brought in Boston in 1849 in behalf of Sarah Roberts, 6, who had to pass five white schools to reach her inferior Negro school. Although represented by Charles Sumner, Sarah Roberts lost her case, but in 1855 continued Negro agitation caused the legislature to order the Boston schools to desegregate.

Northern Negroes were crowded into ghettos, confined to the worst schools and lowest-paying jobs. They were often the objects of rioting by whites who feared their job competition or resented them for the growing agitation over slavery in the American political life. Excluded from many places, Northern Negroes established their own schools, churches, and fraternal organizations and continued to carry on their battle for justice and equal rights. That they met with so little success is a measure of the forces arrayed against them rather than their capacity for resistance.

Bibliography

1. Leon F. Litwack, *North of Slavery: The Negro in the Free States, 1790-1860* (University of Chicago Press, Chicago, 1961, and paperback), is a careful, scholarly examination of the difficulties faced by Northern Negroes by the ante-bellum era. It discusses the emergence of Negro efforts in education, religion, and political life. Chapter II, on the attitude of the federal government toward free Negroes, is fascinating. Recommended for teachers and high school students doing special research. Its bibliographical essay is an important guide to further study of the subject.

2. Langston Hughes and Arna Bontemps, *The Poetry of the Negro, 1746-1949* (Doubleday; New York, 1949), pages 3-11. Includes poems of this era written by free Negro poets. This volume is useful for integrating Negro literature into the course of study and relating it to historical events. Recommended for English and history teachers and high school students.

3. Herbert Aptheker, ed., *A Documentary History of the Negro People in the United States* (Citadel, New York, 1962, and paperback), includes many fascinating documents recounting the Negro's struggle for freedom and justice in the North. It is useful for teachers and high school students.

4. The NAACP booklet, *Negro Heroes of Emancipation* (New York, 1964), includes sketches and biographies of many Negroes who took part in the industrial growth of the North before the Civil War. Readable and useful for teachers or students doing research.

5. Charlotte L. Forten, *The Journal of Charlotte L. Forten* (Collier, New York, 1961, paperback), is the diary of a free Negro teen-ager living in pre-war Boston. Her experiences at school and in the turmoil of Boston anti-slavery politics are often interesting and informative. The annotations by editor Ray Allen

Ira Aldridge grew up in New York City and performed in the Shakespearean dramas of an all-Negro acting troupe. He won fame and fortune from Dublin, Ireland, to St. Petersburg, Russia, but was not allowed to perform in any theater in the slave state of Maryland. *Schomburg Collection, N.Y. Public Library*

Billington supply valuable historical notes and biographical data about the persons mentioned in this young student's exciting life. Recommended for outside reading for high school students.

6. Lavinia Dobler and Edgar A. Toppin, *Pioneers and Patriots* (Doubleday, New York, 1965, and paperback). Chapter 5 is devoted to Paul Cuffee, the Negro merchant and philanthropist. It is a well-written story that includes pictures and is directed toward junior high readers.

7. James M. McPherson, *The Negro's Civil War* (Pantheon, New York, 1965, and paperback). Chapters V, VII, and XVIII, are devoted to the Negro struggle for equality and justice in the North during the Civil War. In a tightly written text and through the selection of interesting documents, McPherson shows how Negroes battled for their rights in meetings and petition campaigns or through direct action. Useful for teachers and high school upperclassmen.

8. Langston Hughes and Milton Meltzer, *A Pictorial History of the Negro in America* (Crown, New York, 1968), pages 68-83. Conveys the plight and success of the Northern free Negro struggling for equality. Useful for teachers and students.

9. Russell L. Adams, *Great Negroes Past and Present* (Afro-American, Chicago, 1964), has sketches and brief biographies of businessmen John Jones, Paul Cuffee, and James Forten, editor Martin R. Delany, and actor Ira Aldridge. Useful for teachers and students doing research.

10. Herbert Marshall and Mildred Stock, *Ira Aldridge, the Negro Tragedian* (Macmillan, New York, 1958), is the story of the New York Negro who became world famous for his renditions of Shakespearean roles. It will be enjoyed by high school students, particularly those interested in drama.

11. Arna Bontemps and Jack Conroy, *Anyplace But Here* (Hill and Wang, New York, 1966, and paperback). Chapter IV is the absorbing story of John Jones, the former slave who became a rich Illinois businessman and devoted his life to the battle against slavery and discrimination. Interesting reading for teachers and high school students.

12. Esther M. Douty, *Forten the Sailmaker* (Rand McNally, Chicago, 1968), is the biography of James Forten, early black philanthropist and abolitionist. Highly recommended to students for outside reading and reports.

13. Frank J. Webb, *The Garies and Their Friends* (Arno Press, New York, 1969), is a reprint of a pre–Civil War black novel about Philadelphia. For students, as outside reading.

14. William Loren Katz, *Eyewitness: The Negro in American History* (Pitman, New York, 1967, and paperback). Chapter VI describes in text, pictures, and eyewitness accounts the plight and progress of the black American in the North. Recommended for students as supplementary reading or an aid to research.

15. Benjamin Quarles, *Black Abolitionists* (Oxford University Press, New York, 1969, and paperback), is a scholarly study of the role of black men and women in the anti-slavery movement.

Sectional Strife Leads to Civil War

Dates to Remember

1829 David Walker's *Appeal,* calling for slave revolts, initiates a militant fight to abolish slavery in America.

1831 William Lloyd Garrison, relying on Negro financiers and readers, begins publication of the *Liberator.*

1841 Frederick Douglass joins the abolitionist movement as a speaker.

1846 Southern expansionists help precipitate a war with Mexico.

1850 The Compromise of 1850 includes a strict Fugitive Slave Law that generates greater Northern resistance.

1859 John Brown leads Negroes and whites in a futile raid on Harper's Ferry, Virginia.

1860 Lincoln is elected President; secession begins.

In the growing crisis over slavery, the Negro played an important role, both as a participant and as a causal factor. The earliest abolitionists were the slaves and the free Negroes who offered them aid. Later the Quakers became the first white group to give help and comfort to the slaves. The militant abolitionist movement can be dated from the 1829 fiery pamphlet of free Negro David Walker, who called for slave uprisings. By 1830 annual Negro conventions met in the North to fight slavery and discrimination. In 1831 William Lloyd Garrison, the first white man to see the problems of slavery as a Negro might, began his *Liberator* and became a rallying point for militant abolitionists of both races.

The most significant Negro leader of this era of crisis was Frederick Douglass, a Maryland slave who escaped to the North. At great personal danger, Douglass became a leading abolitionist speaker, editor, and author of three books telling of his life as a slave and free man. Douglass' interests also included women's rights, Irish freedom, opposition to capital punishment, support for federal aid to education, universal peace, temperance, and civil rights. He played a leading role in the first Women's Rights Convention at Seneca Falls, New York, in 1848 and took part in various European reform movements of the nineteenth century.

The abolitionist movement included Negroes and whites, men and women, direct actionists and moral suasionists. Some whites sought to restrict Negro leaders to symbolic roles, while others insisted on a fully integrated anti-slavery movement. Sojourner Truth, William Wells Brown, Frances Ellen Watkins Harper, Harriet Tubman, and many other Negroes gave the abolitionist movement some of its most important speeches, pamphlets, and arguments. The Underground Railroad, largely a Negro-led enterprise, was actually a reform movement using direct action methods. In each major city of the North these Negro and white abolitionists battled U.S. marshals and local sheriffs to prevent fugitive slaves from being returned to their alleged masters.

By the 1840's anti-slavery activity had the support of the major reformers of the time, including writers Ralph Waldo Emerson and Henry David Thoreau; women's rights advocates Susan B. Anthony, Elizabeth Cady Stanton, and Lucy Stone; educators Horace Mann and Samuel Gridley Howe; and young lawyers Wendell Phillips, Chester A. Arthur, Rutherford B. Hayes, and Richard Henry Dana. It was a world-wide movement that attracted the support of O'Connor in Ireland, Wilberforce in England, and Victor Hugo in France.

The 1850's brought sectional strife to a head. Southern slave-catchers were foiled in the North by abolitionist lawyers or "vigilance committees" that plucked Negro fugitives from the hands of the law. Southern abolitionists were hounded out of their states or killed by lynch mobs. A free Carolina Negro was sentenced to ten years in prison for owning a copy of Harriet Beecher Stowe's *Uncle Tom's Cabin*. The Underground Railroad increased its illegal operations during the 1850-1860 decade, to the rising consternation of Southern masters.

Violence flared in Kansas for years as pro-slavery and anti-slavery settlers battled for control of the government. Senator Charles Sumner, after delivering a scorching anti-slavery speech, was beaten unconscious on the floor of Congress by a South Carolina representative. In 1859 John Brown launched his famous raid on Harper's Ferry and died a martyr on the gallows in Virginia. The Republican party was formed, among other reasons, to combat the extension of slavery to the West. When the slavery issue split the Democrats in 1860, Republican Abraham Lincoln was elected to the presidency and Southern states began to secede.

Bibliography

1. John Hope Franklin, *From Slavery to Freedom* (Knopf, New York, 1967). Chapter XV discusses the worsening crisis over slavery and describes the role played by Negro activists. Useful for teachers and high school upperclassmen.

2. William Loren Katz, *Eyewitness: The Negro in American History* (Pitman, New York, 1967, and paperback). Chapters VII and VIII describe the Negro role in many American reform movements of the ante-bellum period with heavy emphasis on abolitionism. Eyewitness accounts and pictures describe the exciting pre–Civil War years of struggle and violence. Recommended for teachers and students.

3. Herbert Aptheker, ed., *A Documentary History of the Negro People in the United States* (Citadel, New York, 1962), has the most complete documentary collection on the Negro's role in the events leading toward Civil War. It is useful for teachers and high school upperclassmen.

4. Leon Litwack, *North of Slavery* (University of Chicago Press, Chicago, 1961, and paperback). Chapter VII discusses Negro and white abolitionists. Recommended for teachers and high school upperclassmen.

5. John L. Thomas, ed., *Slavery Attacked: The Abolitionist Crusade* (Prentice-Hall, Englewood Cliffs, N.J., 1965, and paperback), is a collection of abolitionist writings and speeches. Particularly valuable is Chapter VII on the Crisis of the 1850's. Useful for teachers and high school upperclassmen.

With the aid of a white Richmond friend, Henry "Box" Brown had himself mailed to Philadelphia. The Underground Railroad united the efforts of Negro and white abolitionists and infuriated slave-holders.

Schomburg Collection, N.Y. Public Library

6. Frederick Douglass, *Life and Times of Frederick Douglass* (Collier, New York, 1962, paperback), is a reprint of the 1892 autobiography of the famed Negro abolitionist and world reformer. Since Douglass' active political life spanned fifty years, this book can be used as a supplement in this and several other units in the course of study. Useful for teachers and high school students.

7. Dorothy Sterling, *Forever Free* (Doubleday, New York, 1963), pages 133-182. Takes the story of the Negro struggle for freedom up to the election of 1860. In a masterly prose style that holds the interest of junior high students, Miss Sterling describes the worsening crisis over slavery in starkly realistic word pictures. Highly recommended for teachers and junior high students.

8. *Walker's Appeal in Four Articles* and *An Address to the Slaves of the United States of America* (Arno Press, New York, 1969, and paperback), is a reprint of David Walker's fiery 1827 call for slave rebellions and Reverend Henry H. Garnet's 1843 speech, also calling for massive slave uprisings. Recommended as a research source for teachers and high school students.

9. John Hope Franklin, *The Militant South* (Harvard University Press, Cambridge, 1956, and Beacon paperback), is the story of Southern violence and filibustering that culminated in the Civil War. This insight into the Southern character is carefully documented with the words of Southern fanatics. It should be useful for teachers and high school upperclassmen.

10. Janet Stevenson, *Sisters and Brothers* (Crown, New York, 1966), is the story of two abolitionist Southern women, the famous Grimke sisters, who find they have two Negro brothers. High school students should find this novel (based upon historical fact) very interesting.

11. Delight Ansley, *The Sword and the Spirit* (Crowell, New York, 1955), is a fast-moving biography of John Brown, the fiery abolitionist who led the raid on Harper's Ferry. Useful for all students.

12. Shirley Graham, *There Was Once a Slave* (Messner, New York, 1947), is the moving story of reformer Frederick Douglass. It is written for secondary school students.

Harriet Tubman, who guided three hundred Negroes to freedom on the Underground Railroad. She served as a scout for the Union Army during the Civil War.
Schomburg Collection, N.Y. Public Library

13. Langston Hughes and Milton Meltzer, *A Pictorial History of the Negro in America* (Crown, New York, 1968). Pages 110-155 depict the growing crisis over slavery and its central ideas and leaders in vivid pictures and clear text. Valuable for research, display, and class use.

14. Ralph Korngold, *Two Friends of Man* (Little, Brown, Boston, 1950), is an excellent dual biography of the two white champions of abolitionism, William Lloyd Garrison and Wendell Phillips. Drawing heavily upon source materials, the author presents a unique picture of these abolitionists' motivations, activities, and impact. Recommended for teachers and as students' outside reading.

15. Dwight Lowell Dumond, *Antislavery* (University of Michigan Press, Ann Arbor, 1961), is the most complete, useful, and scholarly study of the abolitionist movement. It covers the main participants, arguments, and events of this turbulent period. Included with the interesting text are fascinating large pictures taken from contemporary publications. Recommended for teachers and students doing research.

16. Henrietta Buckmaster, *Flight to Freedom: The Story of the Underground Railroad* (Crowell, New York, 1958), is the exciting story of the abolitionists who took direct-action methods to try to end slavery. Recommended for junior high students. This volume is a juvenile version of *Let My People Go* (Harper, New York, 1941, and Beacon paperback), which is recommended for teachers and high school students.

17. The Pepsi-Cola Company's *Adventures in Negro History, Vol. II: The Frederick Douglass Years* is a filmstrip, long-playing record, and script on the years 1817-1895 in the history of the American Negro. The connecting thread is the life of Frederick Douglass, who rose from slavery to world prominence. While much of the information is interesting and well presented, the recording is often disorganized and mixes too many concepts and documentary techniques too quickly for the junior high student to whom it is directed. The last two-thirds could be used to introduce or summarize a unit on abolitionism and Civil War.

18. Richard O. Curry, ed., *The Abolitionists, Reformers or Fanatics?* (Holt, Rinehart & Winston, New York, 1965, paperback), is a series of readings evaluating the efforts of the abolitionists and discussing their origins, leadership, and participation in the growing crisis over slavery. Useful for research by high school students.

19. Louis Filler, *The Crusade Against Slavery, 1830-1860* (Harper, New York, 1960, and paperback), is a careful study of the abolitionist movement, one of the few to include the Negro abolitionists so vital to its success. Useful for high school students doing research.

20. William Still, *The Underground Railroad* (Arno Press, New York, 1968), reprints the only near-complete collection of records of any station on the Underground Railroad. It includes fascinating eyewitness accounts and some fine pictures. Recommended highly for research by teachers and students.

21. Jacqueline Bernard, *Journey Toward Freedom* (Norton, New York, 1967), is the biography of Sojourner Truth, a former New York slave who became a leading abolitionist. It is beautifully told and illustrated, highly recommended for all students as outside reading or research.

22. Howard N. Meyer, *Colonel of the Black Regiment* (Norton, New York, 1967), is the biography of abolitionist Thomas Wentworth Higginson, commander of the first official ex-slave regiment of the Civil War. Highly recommended for high school students.

23. Martin Robison Delany, *The Condition, Elevation, Emigration, and Destiny of the Colored People of the United States* (Arno Press, New York, 1969), reprints a black militant's early history of his people and proposals for change—including an early call for separation from white America. For teachers and high school students doing research.

24. Levi Coffin, *Reminiscences* (Arno Press, New York, 1968), another reprint, contains famous cases of the Underground Railroad by its "reputed president," an Indiana Quaker. Good outside reading for teachers or students and also helpful for research.

25. *The Anglo African Magazine, I* (Arno Press, New York, 1968), is a reprint of a New York black magazine for the crisis year 1859. Useful for research by high school students.

The Civil War

Dates to Remember

1861 Negro volunteers are officially rejected by the Union Army, but by September Negroes have fought in land and sea battles.

1862 Slave Robert Smalls and his Negro crew deliver their Confederate gunboat to the Union Navy outside Charleston.

1863 On New Year's Day Lincoln signs the Emancipation Proclamation.

1863 Negroes are officially accepted in the Union Army and Navy.

1863 Anti-Negro riots, worst racial conflicts in American history, rock New York City, leaving hundreds dead.

1865 As Negro soldiers and civilians demand the right to vote, Lincoln proposes enfranchising Negroes who are veterans or educated.

The Civil War was a turning point for America and its Negro population. Though few Americans knew it at the time, the guns that opened fire on Fort Sumter in 1861 were announcing both the death of American Negro slavery and the rise of Northern industrial power. The American Negro played a vital role during these four crucial years of conflict.

From the beginning of the war, Negroes saw it as their opportunity for freedom, the bluecoats as their liberators. Slaves fled to Union lines offering important manpower and valuable information on enemy positions. Many offered to cook, fight the Confederates, or serve as spies. Despite Union policy that initially demanded that slaves be returned to their Confederate masters, some Union generals made use of the black volunteers. General Ben Butler's declaration in 1861 that the slaves that fled to his lines were "contraband of war" and would not be returned to their Confederate owners, set the legal stage for Lincoln's Emancipation Proclamation. But for a year and a half after the war began, Negroes were denied the right to fight in the armed forces, and the President maintained he had no intention of interfering with slavery.

Lincoln issued the Emancipation Proclamation as Union armies met defeats and their losses mounted. It was born of military necessity and to win back waning European support, rather than as opposition to slavery. As a matter of fact, it freed no slaves: slaves held in areas under Union control were not liberated; those in Confederate regions could not be freed until Northern armies reached them. The Proclamation's important exclusions and its temporary nature made the passage of the Thirteenth Amendment in 1865 imperative to insure real and irrevocable Negro liberty.

Although slaves had served unofficially in the Union armed forces long before Emancipation, the Proclamation formally opened the Army to Negro volunteers. Frederick Douglass and other Negro leaders immediately called on Negroes to join, and more than 200,000 served in the Army and Navy before the war ended. It was first feared that Negroes, particularly those who had been slaves, would make poor soldiers. Lincoln worried about this; Southern newspapers joked about it; many Northerners were skeptical of the Negro's military prowess. But in battle after battle, Negro soldiers held their ground, advanced under fire, and won important victories. Twenty-two won the Medal of Honor for their heroism.

The Negro contribution to Union victory was made despite the most adverse conditions. Negroes received less training, poorer medical care, and shoddier weapons than white troops. Their casualty rate was much higher than that of the whites. They were commanded by white officers who at first doubted their ability. For eighteen months Negro soldiers were granted half the pay given white soldiers; several regiments of Northern Negroes refused all pay until it was equalized by Congress—but continued to fight. In addition, Negro soldiers were informed by the enemy

A Negro soldier asks General Grant to throw away his cigar. More
than 200,000 Negroes served in the Union Army and Navy, and
twenty-two earned the Medal of Honor.
William Loren Katz Collection

that they would be treated as slave rebels if captured, and put to death or sold into slavery. But this only made them more determined fighters.

Throughout the four-year conflict, Negroes battled for their rights as American citizens. They continued their petition campaigns and demonstrations against discriminatory state laws and local segregation practices, particularly in transportation. In Washington, D.C., abolitionist Sojourner Truth refused to move to the Negro section of a streetcar and won her point; in Philadelphia, Negroes finally won desegregation of the streetcar lines after years of campaigning; many states repealed the "Black Laws" that restricted Negro rights; and the federal government began to hire Negro mail carriers and other employees. By 1864 a Negro convention in Syracuse, New York, demanded full manhood rights for all, North and South, Negro and white.

In President Lincoln Negroes had found a friend. He opened the White House to Negro visitors, used Negro advisers, and developed a relationship with Frederick Douglass based on mutual respect. It was a time of hope for black people.

Bibliography

1. James M. McPherson, *The Negro's Civil War* (Pantheon, New York, 1965, and paperback), presents a fascinating picture of what Negroes said and did during the war through eyewitness accounts tied together by important editorial comments and factual information. For teachers. *Marching Toward Freedom,* an excellent children's version of this story, is highly recommended to students for research or outside reading.

2. Rayford W. Logan and Irving S. Cohen, *The American Negro* (Houghton Mifflin, Boston, 1967). Chapter V tells of the part played by black Americans in the Civil War. Recommended for supplementary reading or research by students.

3. Thomas Wentworth Higginson, *Army Life in a Black Regiment* (Beacon and Collier paperbacks), is the story of the first official Negro regiment of the Civil War, told by their commander, an ardent abolitionist. It is an exciting story, and well told. It includes one of the earliest essays on Negro spirituals and an im-

portant appendix of significant documents about Negro troops. Recommended for teachers and high school students.

4. Lerone Bennett, Jr., *Before the Mayflower* (Johnson, Chicago, 1962, 1964, 2d rev. ed., 1969, Pelican paperback). Chapter 7 details the black man's part in the Civil War. Recommended as reference reading by teachers or as supplementary or research reading by students.

5. Dorothy Sterling, *Freedom Train* (Doubleday, New York, 1954), pages 136-177. This book tells of heroine Harriet Tubman's labor for the Union Army during the war. It is followed by documents that confirm the role this gallant woman played in her nation's defense. Recommended for junior high students.

6. Peter Burchard, *One Gallant Rush* (St. Martin's, New York, 1965), is the story of the 54th Regiment, U.S. Colored Troops, and their white commander, Colonel Robert Shaw. Recommended for high school students' outside reading.

7. Charlotte L. Forten, *The Journal of Charlotte L. Forten* (Collier, New York, 1961, paperback). Chapters 6 and 7 detail the young Negro teacher's role in instructing former slaves in the Georgia Sea Islands during the war, a realistic picture of Negro self-help at this time. This book should appeal to high school students.

8. Dorothy Sterling, *Captain of the Planter* (Doubleday, New York, 1958), is the story of Robert Smalls, the Negro pilot who delivered his Confederate gunboat to the Union Navy and later served five terms as a South Carolina congressman. It is well written, has excellent pictures, and is carefully researched. Excellent reading for junior high students.

9. Mimi Cooper Levy, *Corrie and the Yankee* (Viking, New York, 1959), is a novel of Negro resistance to slavery and support for Union soldiers during the Civil War. It is an interesting story, whose main character is a child. Recommended for junior high students.

10. The McGraw-Hill movie *1861-1877: Civil War and Reconstruction* covers the Negro role in the war and the attempt at Reconstruction that followed it. Its pictures are excellent, the text terse and exciting. Most useful as an overview of the period, this twenty-minute black-and-white documentary should have appeal

for junior and senior high students and should be followed by a summary.

11. The McGraw-Hill filmstrip *The Negro in Civil War and Reconstruction* covers the same topics as the movie but in color frames, and allows the teacher more time for depth treatment of the various topics. Like the others in this series, it is carefully constructed for classroom use and should be interesting for students.

12. John Hope Franklin, *The Emancipation Proclamation* (Doubleday, New York, 1963, and paperback), details the background events and meaning of the first presidential order to affect American Negroes. Useful for teachers and high school upperclassmen.

13. Richard C. Wade, ed., *The Negro in American Life* (Houghton Mifflin, Boston, 1965). Chapter IV illuminates, through selected documents, the black man's part in the Civil War. Recommended for reading and research by teachers and students.

14. Dudley Taylor Cornish, *The Sable Arm* (Norton, New York, 1956, and paperback), is the full story of Negro troops in the Union Army. Recommended for teachers and high school upperclassmen, particularly for research.

15. Langston Hughes and Milton Meltzer, *A Pictorial History of the Negro in America* (Crown, New York, 1963), pages 154-185. Tells the story of the Negro's role in the Civil War in striking photographs and drawings made at the time. Recommended for teachers and students.

16. Irvin H. Lee, *Negro Medal of Honor Men* (Dodd, Mead, New York, 1967). Chapter III is the story of twenty Negroes who won the Medal of Honor during the Civil War. Recommended for junior and senior high school readers.

17. James M. McPherson, *The Struggle for Equality: Abolitionists and the Negro in the Civil War and Reconstruction* (Princeton University Press, Princeton, 1964, and paperback), is a carefully documented study of Negro and abolitionist efforts to achieve racial equality during and after the Civil War. Scholarly, informative, and interesting, this volume should be of great aid to senior high students doing research.

A poster recruiting Negro troops for the Civil War. Frederick
Douglass and other Negro leaders were among the main recruiters.
Schomburg Collection, N.Y. Public Library

18. Susie King Taylor, *Reminiscences of My Life in Camp* (Arno Press, New York, 1968), is a reprint of the autobiography of a black Civil War nurse. Recommended as outside reading for students.

19. William Loren Katz, *Eyewitness: The Negro in American History* (Pitman, New York, 1967, and paperback). Chapter 9 tells of the black man's part in the Civil War through text, pictures, and eyewitness accounts. For teachers or students.

Reconstruction, 1865-1877

Traditionally historians have pictured the Negro as bewildered by freedom, a helpless tool of Northern carpetbaggers, unsuited to vote or hold office, and the passive pawn in the depraved "era of Reconstruction." The record of the Southern Negro stands in sharp contrast to these durable myths.

Upon his emancipation, the Negro searched for loved ones separated from him during slavery and began to seek a job, a home, some security, and an education. While Negroes appeared quite content to forget and forgive slaveowners, the white response to Negro freedom in the South was one of fear and hatred. Negroes were restricted by Black Codes that replaced the Slave Codes. In Mississippi the word *slave* was simply changed to *Negro* and the old Slave Code re-enacted. Under these laws Negroes found they could not enter skilled occupations, own businesses, buy city land, or exercise their civil rights. Unemployed Negro men and boys were arrested by the sheriff and rented out to their former owners. There was no legal recourse.

In the face of this resurgence of Confederate power and the lack of concern by President Andrew Johnson, congressional leaders Thaddeus Stevens and Charles Sumner demanded a thorough reconstruction of Southern state governments, punishment of Confederate leaders, and citizenship rights for Negroes. The aims of these "radicals" included a mixture of patriotism, sympathy for the Negro, and the desire for Republican party dominance in the South and the nation. By 1868, and under the protection of federal troops, Negroes and poor whites rewrote their state constitutions to guarantee equal rights for all, and to expand public services for the poor and education for all.

The new state constitutions and the governments that followed them brought far-reaching reforms to the South. Roads, schools, libraries, hospitals, and bridges were built; imprisonment for debt was eliminated; women were granted new rights; and civil rights were given to black and white alike. Negroes were elected to local, state, and national offices—Negro lieutenant-governors served in South Carolina, Mississippi, and Louisiana; Negro sheriffs enforced local law even in Mississippi; and the Negro Mayor of Natchez ruled white and black with an even-handed justice. But in no state of the old Confederacy were Negroes ever a majority in the legislature or in control of the reins of government.

Eight of the Southern states elected Negroes to Congress in the years after the Civil War. Half of the twenty-two Negro congressmen were former slaves; most of them had some education and several had been to college. They were all Republicans, as were most Negro voters of this time, and served creditably in the national legislature. None was ever involved in the financial scandals that marked the Grant administration.

Seven of the fourteen Negroes who represented Southern districts during congressional Reconstruction (1868-1876) of the South. They were earnest, hard-working legislators who pursued the best interests of their states and constituents.
Schomburg Collection, N.Y. Public Library

During Reconstruction, Southern Negroes sought unsuccessfully to establish their economic independence through land ownership. The federal government, generous in giving out Western land to railroads and settlers, left the Southern Negro landless and thus in the power of his former owners. Those who proposed a democratic land distribution in the South were considered visionaries or revolutionists, though the failure to provide the Negro with land left him, said Frederick Douglass, "on his knees."

Lacking economic power and therefore at the mercy of the white employer, the Negro was dependent on federal forces for protection. Sheriffs had disarmed Negroes and left the Ku Klux Klan and other anti-Negro organizations armed. Northern businessmen, interested in resuming economic ties with Southern planters, urged the federal government to relax its grip on the South and return it to "home rule"—which meant white supremacy. The meager force of 25,000 federal troops was gradually withdrawn from the South. Klan violence effectively suppressed Negro voters; Negro officials were murdered with impunity; white supporters were warned to desert their Negro allies or face death. In the compromise that settled the election of 1876, President Hayes agreed to remove the last troops from the South. Home rule was restored; white supremacy reigned.

The debacle of Reconstruction can only be understood in terms of the shifting economic and political positions of the North. It was an era of unbridled corruption, massive industrial growth, and changing moral values. The new hero was the industrial giant, not the starry-eyed abolitionist. Negroes and every other issue were second to economic gain. The Fourteenth Amendment, designed to protect Negro citizenship, was instead used to shield corporations from government interference. The Northern businessman was obviously more interested in making money than in insuring the former slave his new rights. In an age that made heroes of Horatio Alger and Jim Fiske, few wanted to hear about the persecution of the lowly.

Bibliography

1. Kenneth M. Stampp, *The Era of Reconstruction, 1865-1877*

(Knopf, New York, 1965, and Vintage paperback), discusses the truths and fables of Reconstruction history and historiography in a fact-laden and important book. Recommended for teachers wishing an accurate survey of the period, and for high school upperclassmen doing research.

2. Herbert Aptheker, ed., *A Documentary History of the Negro People in the United States* (Citadel, New York, 1962, paperback). Chapter 5 is the most thorough collection of Negro writing available for this period. Congressional testimony, speeches, letters, and petitions are included in their entirety. Useful for research by teachers and high school upperclassmen.

3. Milton Meltzer, *In Their Own Words,* Vol. II (Crowell, New York, 1965, and paperback), includes almost a hundred pages of text and documents by Negroes during Reconstruction. The documents have been carefully selected and edited, and the text includes pictures. Useful for high school students despite a preoccupation with sheer brutality.

4. John Hope Franklin, *From Slavery to Freedom* (Knopf, New York, 1967). Chapters XVII and XVIII present a balanced view of Reconstruction in the South, its accomplishments and shortcomings, and its eventual overthrow by the forces of white supremacy. There is much detailed information here for teachers and high school upperclassmen.

5. William Loren Katz, *Eyewitness: The Negro in American History* (Pitman, New York, 1967, and paperback). Chapters X and XI present documents, pictures, and text describing the Negro's trials and triumphs during Reconstruction, including many previously unpublished eyewitness accounts by Negroes and whites. Recommended for teachers and students.

6. Grady McWhiney, *Reconstruction and the Freedmen* (Rand McNally, Chicago, 1963, paperback), is an excellent and brief series of documents on the Negro's role in the political, economic, and social life of Reconstruction. Recommended for teachers and high school students.

7. Richard N. Current, ed., *Reconstruction* (Prentice-Hall, Englewood Cliffs, N.J., 1965, paperback), is a carefully organized collection of documents on Reconstruction by Southerners (Negro

and white) and Northerners. Each section and each document has
an introduction providing information about its historical content.
Recommended for teachers and high school students.

8. Vernon Lane Wharton, *The Negro in Mississippi, 1865-
1890* (University of North Carolina Press, Chapel Hill, 1947, and
paperback), is a scholarly study of the Negro's role in Mississippi
life during and after Reconstruction. Chapter IV on the Freedmen's Bureau and Chapter V on the Black Codes are excellent
for research. Recommended for teachers and high school students.

9. Frederick Douglass, *Life and Times of Frederick Douglass*
(Collier, New York, 1962, paperback). Chapters 13 and 14 present the recollections of the outstanding Negro leader of the period
(and an important participant in the events of the time). Douglass
sheds interesting light on the character and role of President
Andrew Johnson and his efforts to deal with Negro demands for
equality. Useful for teachers and high school students doing
research.

10. Howard Fast, *Freedom Road* (Duell, Sloan, New York,
1944, and several paperbacks), is an excellent novel of Negro
effort during Reconstruction. Set in post-Civil War South Carolina,
this story of fictional Gideon Jackson is stimulating outside reading for secondary school students.

11. The McGraw-Hill movie and filmstrip mentioned in the
bibliography of Unit VII (Civil War) are applicable in this unit.

12. Langston Hughes and Milton Meltzer, *A Pictorial History
of the Negro in America* (Crown, New York, 1968), pages 186-
214. Describes in vivid pictures and clear text the Negro contributions to Reconstruction. These pictures and accounts of Negro
leaders should be particularly useful for junior high classes, and
teachers should find the information and approach most helpful.

13. Russell L. Adams, *Great Negroes Past and Present* (Afro-
American, Chicago, 1964). Section III includes sketches and
short biographies of the main Negro figures of the Reconstruction
period, including most of the black congressmen. The pictures are
useful for class display, the text valuable for teachers and students.
This is the best collection of Negro Reconstruction biographies
available.

14. The NAACP booklet, *Negro Heroes of Emancipation,* also contains short biographies of Negro leaders of the Civil War and Reconstruction periods: John Jones; Frederick Douglass; Hiram R. Revels (Mississippi senator); Frances Ellen Watkins Harper (poet); John Mercer Langston (diplomat); Congressmen Henry McNeal Turner, Robert Smalls, Robert Brown Elliott, and Blanche K. Bruce (a Mississippi senator). This biographical collection includes pictures and should be useful to junior high students doing research.

15. W. E. B. DuBois, *Black Reconstruction* (Harcourt Brace, New York, 1935, and Meridian paperback), is a provocative study of the postwar period by the famous Negro historian. Despite its tendency to easy generalization, this book is useful for its many quotes and state-by-state analysis of Negro accomplishments. Useful to teachers and high school students doing research.

16. Carol F. Drisko and Edgar A. Toppin, *The Unfinished March* (Doubleday, New York, 1967, and paperback). Chapters One to Three are an excellent summary of Reconstruction for junior high readers. Major concepts are clearly explained and text and pictures attractive for this reading level.

17. Willie Lee Rose, *Rehearsal for Construction* (Bobbs-Merrill, Indianapolis, 1964, and Vintage paperback), is the prizewinning study of the Port Royal experiment in reconstruction that began during the Civil War. Scholarly, fascinating, and well written, this book is an important study of whites as well as Negroes during this crucial stage in American racial relations. Its availability in paperback is an important contribution to our schools. Highly recommended for teachers and high school students, particularly for research in Reconstruction.

18. Lerone Bennett, Jr., *Black Power, U.S.A.: The Human Side of Reconstruction* (Johnson, Chicago, 1967, and paperback), is a hard-hitting version of Reconstruction history with particular emphasis on crucial power relationships. The book should be helpful to high school students, either for outside reading or for research, and to teachers doing further work in this field.

19. Alan Conway, *The Reconstruction of Georgia* (University of Minnesota Press, Minneapolis, 1966), is a valuable scholarly

study of Georgia by a Welsh historian who did his research in the state. One of the few recent studies of a Southern state during Reconstruction, it is a valuable contribution toward understanding what went wrong in Southern racial relations. Recommended for senior high school students doing research.

20. Walter L. Fleming, ed., *Documentary History of Reconstruction* (McGraw-Hill, New York, 1966, paperback), is a reprint of a classic, two-volume collection of Reconstruction documents. The work is heavily weighted in favor of the old Southern aristocracy and against the freedmen. Volume I covers the period of Presidential Reconstruction; Volume II covers Radical Reconstruction and its downfall. Students might profitably contrast its selection with that of the Meltzer and Aptheker volumes previously mentioned. Recommended for research by senior high students.

21. Richard C. Wade, ed., *The Negro in American Life* (Houghton Mifflin, Boston, 1965). Chapter 5 uses several documents to detail the Negro's role in Reconstruction. Useful for research.

22. William A. Sinclair, *The Aftermath of Slavery* (Arno Press, New York, 1969, and paperback), is the reprint of a neglected black historian's vital evaluation of Reconstruction. For teachers' and students' research.

23. Elizabeth Ware Pearson, ed., *Letters from Port Royal* (Arno Press, New York, 1969, and paperback), reprints letters from America's first freedom schools in the South after the Civil War. Recommended for both teachers and students.

24. John R. Lynch, *The Facts of Reconstruction* (Arno Press, New York, 1968, and paperback), a reprint, is the black Mississippi Congressman's incisive analysis of Reconstruction. Recommended for teachers and high school students doing research on the period.

25. Lydia Maria Child, *The Freedman's Book* (Arno Press, New York, 1968), is a reprinted children's text designed for ex-slaves in the South. For outside reading.

The Growth of Industry and Labor

Dates to Remember

1869 First convention of the National Colored Labor Union.

1883 Jan Matzeliger invents a lasting machine that revolutionizes the shoe industry.

1900 Booker T. Washington begins the National Negro Business League.

1923 Garrett A. Morgan invents the automatic traffic light.

1925 A. Philip Randolph organizes the Negro Pullman Porters' Union.

The tremendous industrial thrust that followed the Civil War benefited from the inventions of many Negroes and whites. By 1913, the fiftieth anniversary of the Emancipation Proclamation, an estimated thousand inventions had been patented by American Negroes, many in the important fields of industrial machinery, electrical equipment, and rapid transportation.

The most significant inventors of this period were Elijah Mc-Coy, Jan Matzeliger, Granville T. Woods, Lewis Latimer, and Garrett A. Morgan. McCoy, born to slave parents who escaped to Canada via the Underground Railroad, held more than fifty patents. His most significant contribution was the lubricating cup that fed oil to machinery without halting its operation. It was used in ships, trains, and factories. Granville T. Woods held over thirty-five patents on devices sold to American Bell Telephone, General Electric, and Westinghouse Air Brake. He developed an automatic air brake and a system for communicating between moving trains, and contributed to the development of the "third rail."

Jan Matzeliger, a poor Lynn, Massachusetts, shoemaker, developed a machine that virtually revolutionized the shoe industry. Like other Negro inventors, Matzeliger was unable to market his invention and sold it to the United Shoe Company, for which it was the basis of a gigantic financial growth. Lewis Latimer worked alongside Alexander Graham Bell and made the patent drawings for Bell's first telephone. He then went on to work for Thomas Edison, wrote a book explaining the electrical system to the public, and served as Edison's star witness in many patent cases. Garrett A. Morgan invented the gas mask used by American troops in World War I and later developed the automatic traffic light that brought increased safety to the nation's streets and highways.

Negro business efforts often met overwhelming white resistance. But segregation led to the development of Negro businesses serving Negro areas and the introduction by Negroes of products that appealed specifically to their people. Madame C. J. Walker became a millionaire by perfecting beauty preparations for Negro women. The National Negro Business League sought to encourage Negro enterprises and claimed hundreds of chapters by 1910. By the turn of the century there were Negro insurance companies and banks serving a Negro clientele ignored by whites. By the mid-twentieth century some of these had become multi-million-dollar enterprises employing thousands of workers.

Labor unions became the first major American organizations in the post-Civil War period to exclude Negroes. The National Labor Union first admitted Negroes and then suggested that they form separate locals. Negro unionist Isaac Myers formed the National Colored Labor Union and worked long hours to make it a powerful labor organization. His efforts failed because, he pointed out, Negro and white workers must unite in order to withstand the power of their employers. The Knights of Labor admitted Negroes, hired Negro organizers and soon boasted sixty thousand Negro members. But the decline of the organization nationally and its persecution in the Southern states because of its interracial policy ended this hopeful experiment in biracial unionism.

The American Federation of Labor did not exclude Negroes but eventually allowed its member unions to exclude them or place them in segregated locals. The A.F. of L. policy of admitting only skilled laborers virtually excluded most Negroes of the time, for Negroes had not been permitted to learn key skills or take part in apprentice programs. The only union that did not discriminate against Negroes was the United Mine Workers; two-thirds of all Negroes in unions belonged to this one union.

Deprived of learning skills, isolated from the trade unions by one method or another, the Negro was often cast in the role of strikebreaker. This made white laborers even more bitterly anti-Negro. Exclusion from unions also put the Negro in a position where, in order to get and hold a job, he had to work for lower wages than whites—which further angered white workers. The labor movement and Negroes thus shared the suffering caused by union discrimination.

Bibliography

1. Russell L. Adams, *Great Negroes Past and Present* (Afro-American, Chicago, 1964). Chapter IV presents an overview of the Negro in the field of invention and business. Through pictures and brief biographies it presents valuable information on inventors Jan Matzeliger, Granville T. Woods, and Garrett A. Morgan, and business figures Madame C. J. Walker, Maggie Walker, C. C. Spaulding, and A. G. Gaston, among others. Recommended for both teachers and students.

2. *A 1966 Calendar of Inventions and Discoveries,* published by the Carver Federal Savings and Loan Association in New York City, includes pictures and text describing the major Negro inventors of the pre-Civil War period (Banneker, Blair, Temple, Rillieux) and the postwar period (McCoy, Morgan, Latimer, Matzeliger, Woods, and Drew). A brief but important contribution to this neglected field. Recommended for teachers and students.

3. Rayford W. Logan, *The Negro in American Life and Thought, 1877-1901* (Dial, New York, 1954), and *The Betrayal of the Negro* (Collier, New York, 1965, paperback). Chapter 8 details the Negro's painful efforts to enter the American trade union movement after the Civil War. This carefully documented

presentation should be useful to teachers and high school upper-classmen doing research.

4. Ray Stannard Baker, *Following the Color Line* (Harper, New York, 1964, paperback), is a reprint of the famous turn-of-the-century study of the Negro in America by a sensitive white reporter. Part II has some impressions of Negro labor at this time. Recommended for teachers and high school students doing research.

5. Arna Bontemps and Jack Conroy, *Anyplace But Here* (Hill and Wang, New York, 1966), pages 135-147. Tells the story of some of the Negro's efforts and frustrations in uniting with white laboring men after Reconstruction. Recommended for high school students.

6. William Loren Katz, *Eyewitness: The Negro in American History* (Pitman, New York, 1967, and paperback). Chapter 12 is the illustrated story of Negro inventors, laborers, and union leaders and their place in the postwar industrial expansion. The eyewitness section includes some accounts of Negro inventive genius and union activity never published before.

7. Sterling D. Spero and Abram L. Harris, *The Black Worker* (Columbia University Press, New York, 1931), is a survey of the problems and advances of Negro labor before the Great Depression. The appendix includes some interesting documents. Recommended for teachers and high school students doing research.

8. Carter G. Woodson and Charles H. Wesley, *The Negro in Our History* (Associated Publishers, Washington, D.C., 1962), pages 458-467. A textbook treatment of Negro inventors and businessmen of this period. Useful for factual information for teachers and all students.

9. Herbert Hill, *The Racial Practices of Organized Labor— In the Age of Gompers and After* (NAACP, New York, 1965). An interesting and documented study of Negro discrimination in the formative years of the American Federation of Labor. Recommended for high school students and teachers.

10. *Makers of the U.S.A.* (Friendship Press, New York, 1963), is a "pictomap" displaying the contributions to the growth of our country by America's many minorities. It shows pictures of various

Lewis Latimer, inventor, who worked with Thomas Edison and Alexander Graham Bell, drew up the plans for Bell's first telephone.
Schomburg Collection, N.Y. Public Library

nationalities, including Negroes, at work, in the sections of the country where they settled. Suitable for permanent display.

11. Roy Cook, *Leaders of Labor* (Lippincott, Philadelphia, 1966). Chapter XI is devoted to Negro leader A. Philip Randolph. It is a well-written piece of interest to junior and senior high students.

12. *Ingenious Americans,* Old Taylor Distillery Company of Kentucky, is a small booklet relating the story of six Negro inventors, and is available free of charge from the company. Useful for students and teachers.

13. Louis Haber, *The Role of the American Negro in the Fields of Science* (unpublished manuscript, 1966, available from Division of Elementary and Secondary Education, Bureau of Research, Office of Education, Washington, D.C. 20202; refer to author, title, and Project No. 6-8353), summarizes the lives and accomplishments of the major Negro inventors, as well as biologists, chemists, and physicians. It has the most complete bibliography of works about Negroes in science available today.

14. E. Franklin Frazier, *Black Bourgeoisie* (Collier, New York, 1962, and other paperback editions), is the interesting study of Negro business efforts since slavery days. Written by the foremost Negro sociologist of recent times, it explores the nature and power of Negro wealth in America. Recommended highly for senior high school students doing research.

15. Henry E. Baker, *The Colored Inventor* (Arno Press, New York, 1969), is the reprint of a definitive, illustrated booklet on black inventors written fifty years after slave emancipation. Useful for teachers' or students' research or for outside reading.

16. *Iron Horses and Iron Men* (Rediscovery Films, *New York Times,* New York, 1969), is an excellent 16-minute sound movie about the black men whose inventions contributed to the development of railroads and about the efforts of A. Philip Randolph to organize Pullman porters into a union. Highly recommended for all students working on this unit.

17. Julius Jacobson, ed., *The Negro and the American Labor Movement* (Anchor Books, New York, 1968, paperback). Chapters I-V tell of the part played by blacks in pre-Depression labor

unions and of the attitude of white unionists toward them. For teachers and for senior high school students doing research.

18. John Hope Franklin, *From Slavery to Freedom* (Knopf, New York, 1967, and paperback). Pages 400-404 describe efforts of blacks in business, invention, and unions. For research by teachers and senior high school students.

The Last Frontier of Farmers and Cowboys

Dates to Remember

1876 Negro Cowboy Nat Love wins three contests in the Deadwood Rodeo to earn the title of "Deadwood Dick."

1875 First Kentucky Derby has thirteen Negro jockeys out of fourteen.

1879 In a great exodus thousands of blacks leave the South for Kansas and points west.

1890 The Colored Farmers' Alliance reaches a membership of one million.

1892 The Populist party, welcoming' Negro votes, breaks the one-party system in the South.

1901 George H. White of North Carolina, last Negro to be elected from the South, leaves Congress.

In 1900, 90 per cent of America's Negroes still lived in the South, usually on farms they did not own. They were sharecroppers who paid for the land they farmed with a large portion of their crops. Most were hopelessly in debt, for the landlord kept the books and insisted that all major supplies be purchased from him at his prices. Other Negroes were even worse off, caught in the net of Southern injustice and forced to labor for the state or white men to whom the state rented them. These were the convict laborers, Negroes arrested for minor crimes (or none at all), and placed in labor gangs to serve out long sentences. To eliminate political opposition to this oppression, Negro voters were disfranchised by Southern election chicanery or sheer terror. To prevent the rise of a Negro leadership class, Negro education was reduced to a minimum. Southern governors thought educated Negroes were "more dangerous than dynamite."

The farmers' problems of falling prices, rising railroad rates, higher interest rates, and increased cost of farm machinery fell even heavier on the Negro farmer. He was black as well as poor, and he could expect neither sympathy nor justice from sheriff, jury, or judge. As farmers turned to greater cooperation in the Grange and Farmers' Alliances, Negro farmers also united to fight their common enemies. The Colored Farmers' Alliance united a million Negro farmers and was often asked to act in concert with the white Farmers' Alliance.

By the 1890's the farmers of both races had turned to political action and soon found a home in the Populist party. White Populist Tom Watson campaigned in Georgia with Negro leaders. They were guarded by armed white farmers as they urged black and white farmers to unite against their common enemies. Throughout the South, Negroes served on Populist party executive boards and were elected to local and state offices. Negroes played an important role in the 1896 Populist convention at St. Louis and in the election that followed. Perhaps the most significant Negro political figure to emerge from the fusion politics of this time was George H. White, who was twice elected (1896 and 1898) to Congress from North Carolina.

The Negro Populists paid a fearful price for their racial egalitarianism. Terror and murder again swept the South and lynchings reached a peak of four a week by 1892. Bigots played on white fears of "Negro domination" with skill and effectiveness. From 1890 to 1910 each state of the old Confederacy systematically and legally disfranchised its black citizens. The devices included the Grandfather Clause, literacy tests, poll taxes, white primaries, and a series of voters' tests. It was during this period that local and state segregation laws were passed. By the early twentieth century one Southern white triumphantly announced that the Negro had ceased to be "a political factor."

Negroes also played an important part in Western history. Many had been brought West as bondsmen and were cowboys before they became free men. Almost a third of the trail crews that drove cattle up the Chisholm Trail after the Civil War were Negroes. In 1879 one of the greatest migrations to reach the West was made up of thousands of ragged Negroes fleeing Southern oppression and seeking new opportunity in Kansas.

Although neglected by Hollywood movies of the Wild West, Negroes were among those whose actions made them famous or infamous on the frontier. Nat Love rode with the James gang and Billy the Kid, and personally knew Bat Masterson and Buffalo Bill. He was one of the many Negro and white cowboys who shot up Dodge City and Tombstone and points west. Some were killers cut in the mold of Billy the Kid, and they died as he did—in the violence they created.

Negro units of the United States Army did their part to keep the peace. Negro cavalrymen constituted 20 per cent of the total U.S. Cavalry force on the frontier. The Ninth and Tenth Cavalry and Twenty-fourth and Twenty-fifth Infantry patrolled the West from the Rio Grande to the Canadian border, fighting outlaws, Apache, Comanche, and Sioux. Fifteen black soldiers won the Congressional Medal of Honor during these last Indian wars. And the scout Isaiah Dorman rode to fame and death with General Custer at the Little Big Horn.

Bibliography

1. William Loren Katz, *Eyewitness: The Negro in American History* (Pitman, New York, 1967, and paperback). Chapter 13 uses documents, pictures, and text to record the Negro's role on the last frontier and his oppression as a Southern landless farmer. Stories of Negro Western bad men, Populists, and military heroes of the frontier are told in the words of the men who made the history. Recommended for teachers and students.

2. Philip Durham and Everett L. Jones, *The Negro Cowboys* (Dodd, Mead, New York, 1965), is the buried history of the Negroes who rode the Western trails after the Civil War. An excellent job of original research into Western Americana; the text and photographs are attractive for all ages. *The Adventures of the Negro Cowboys* (Dodd, Mead, New York, 1966, and paper-

The 9th and 10th Negro Cavalry Regiments of the U.S. Army made up 20 per cent of the nation's cavalry commitment in the post-Civil War West. Their white scouts included Buffalo Bill, Kit Carson, and Wild Bill Hickok; their enemies included Geronimo, Sitting Bull, and Billy the Kid.
The National Archives

back) is the authors' adaption of this book for young readers. Delightful reading and interesting pictures for children in junior high or elementary school.

3. Rayford W. Logan, *The Betrayal of the Negro* (Collier, New York, 1965, paperback), pages 98-101. Discusses the post-Reconstruction group of Southern Negro congressmen, particularly George H. White, the last one. Recommended for teachers and high school students.

4. Arna Bontemps and Jack Conroy, *Anyplace But Here* (Hill and Wang, New York, 1966). Chapter V is the exciting story of the black "Exodus of 1879" and of the fruitless Southern efforts to halt this mass Negro migration to the West. Recommended for teachers and students.

5. C. Vann Woodward, *The Strange Career of Jim Crow* (Oxford University Press, New York, 1957, and Galaxy paperback), is the history of the Jim Crow laws that came with the Negro's second rise to influence during the post-Reconstruction period of farmer unrest. Recommended for teachers and high school upperclassmen doing special research.

6. C. Vann Woodward, *Tom Watson, Agrarian Rebel* (Macmillan, New York, 1938, and Galaxy paperback), is the story of the white Georgian who led the Georgia Populists into a coalition with the Negroes and later became America's most determined racist. This prize-winning autobiography throws light on the genesis and development of Southern racist thinking.

7. Herschel V. Cachin and others, *Under Fire with the Tenth U.S. Cavalry* (Arno Press, New York, 1969), is a reprint of the profusely illustrated history of black troopers on the frontier and in the Spanish-American War. For teachers' and students' outside reading and research. T. G. Steward, *The Colored Regulars in the United States Army* (Arno Press, New York, 1969), covers the black troopers in the West. For student research.

8. Fairfax Downey, *The Buffalo Soldiers* (McGraw-Hill, New York, 1969), is a story of black troopers during the Indian wars written for junior high school readers. Highly recommended as outside reading for students of this age.

9. Ray Stannard Baker, *Following the Color Line* (Harper, New York, 1964, paperback). Part I is a white reporter's view of the Southern Negro's conditions at the turn of the century. By citing specific examples and using photographs to document his study, reporter Baker presents a realistic picture of the Negro's oppression during this period. Useful for teachers and high school students. Recommended for supplementary reading or research.

10. W. E. B. DuBois, *The Souls of Black Folk* (Crest, New York, 1961, paperback). Chapter VII is the famous Negro leader's impressions of his visits to rural Georgia. Like Baker's, this is a highly personalized account of the Negro's oppression. Useful for teachers and high school upperclassmen.

11. Shirley Graham and George D. Liscomb, *Dr. George Washington Carver, Scientist* (Messner, New York, 1965, and paperback), is the biography of the slave boy who rose to become one of America's most important agricultural scientists. It is one of many biographies of Dr. Carver and is directed toward junior high school readers.

12. *The Life and Adventures of Nat Love* (Arno Press, New York, 1968) is the reprint of a black cowboy's boastful autobiography, with a new introduction. For research.

13. George Brown Tindall, *South Carolina Negroes, 1877-1900* (Louisiana State University Press, 1966, paperback), is a reprint of the 1952 scholarly study of post-Reconstruction Negro life in South Carolina. It covers the Negro farmer, the nullification of the Fifteenth Amendment and equal rights, violence, Negro education, and churches. Recommended for teachers and high school upperclassmen.

14. Carol F. Drisko and Edgar A. Toppin, *The Unfinished March* (Doubleday, New York, 1967, and paperback). Chapter 4 tells of the Southern Negro farmer's plight after Reconstruction and of the Negro cowboys who helped build the West. Recommended for junior high students.

15. William H. Leckie, *The Buffalo Soldiers* (University of Oklahoma Press, Norman, 1967), is the interesting, definitive study of the Negro cavalrymen who helped tame the West. It is

based on extensive research and is valuable for all students doing research on the topic.

16. Timothy Thomas Fortune, *Black and White: Land, Labor and Politics in the South* (Arno Press, New York, 1968, and paperback), reprints a black Populist's evaluation of the South. Highly recommended for high school students' research.

17. Irvin H. Lee, *Negro Medal of Honor Men* (Dodd, Mead, New York, 1967). Chapter 5 is the story of the Negro soldiers stationed in the Western territories who tried to hold down the lawless and the Indians during the days of the last frontier. Specifically, the author tells the story of fourteen Negroes who earned the Congressional Medal of Honor fighting Apaches, Comanches, and outlaws. Recommended for all students and for research.

An Era of Reform and Progress, 1890-1916

Dates to Remember

1892 Negro journalist Ida B. Wells launches an anti-lynching campaign in Memphis, Tennessee, and is forced to flee.

1893 Dr. Daniel Hale Williams performs the first successful operation on the human heart.

1895 Educator Booker T. Washington delivers his historic speech at Atlanta known as "The Atlanta Compromise."

1896 The Supreme Court rules segregation laws do not violate the United States Constitution if facilities are equal.

1909 Commander Robert E. Peary and Matthew Henson reach the North Pole.

1909 Birth of the National Association for the Advancement of Colored People (NAACP), organized by Negro and white reformers.

1910 Birth of the National Urban League to promote job and urban opportunities for Negroes.

The era of reform and progressivism that brought many advances to American life in the decades before World War I left the Negro still mired in discriminatory laws and practices. Neither the reforms of Presidents Cleveland, Roosevelt, or Taft, nor the "New Freedom" of President Wilson had much meaning for American Negroes. Segregation was declared constitutional by the Supreme Court in 1896—and there were more lynchings of Negroes than during any previous decade. The wave of Negro political power during the Populist era left a wake of white resentment. Presidential candidates of both parties always sought Southern white votes at the expense of Negro rights.

During these uneasy years Negro leaders sought to advance their people through a series of accommodations and protests. Ida Wells, an editor of the Memphis *Free Speech,* launched an anti-lynching campaign that took her around the country and the world. In 1900 Negro Congressman George White introduced America's first anti-lynching bill, only to see it die in the House Judiciary Committee. Negro boycotts of segregated streetcars in several Southern cities were a reminder that Negroes did not intend to settle for second-class citizenship. In several Southern towns armed Negroes prevented lynchers from murdering Negroes accused of crimes.

But the outstanding Negro figure of this period was Booker T. Washington, a former slave who sought a *modus vivendi* with Southern whites based on Negro acceptance of segregation in return for greater educational opportunities. His approach was welcomed by most whites and many Negroes, and he soon became an important American political force. Philanthropists channeled their money for Negro education through him and Presidents sought (and followed) his advice on Southern political appointments, Negro and white. Washington stressed manual training schools for Negroes and rejected all agitation against second-class citizenship (although he privately financed legal battles against Jim Crow rules). He believed that Negroes would advance as they increased their economic usefulness to society.

Militants continued to appeal to the Negro masses during the "age of Booker T. Washington." William Monroe Trotter, fiery editor of the *Boston Guardian,* and W. E. B. DuBois, first Negro Ph.D. from Harvard, soon challenged Washington's philosophy and demanded full citizenship rights, including the right to vote. In 1905 DuBois's "Niagara Movement" launched a campaign for complete equality and justice, with emphasis on political rights. In 1909, after an outbreak of rioting and murders against Negroes in Springfield, Illinois, home town of Abraham Lincoln, a protest meeting in New York led to the formation of the NAACP. The new organization had the support of DuBois, Trotter, Wells, and leading white reformers Lincoln Steffens, Ray Stannard Baker, Oswald Garrison Villard, John Dewey, William Dean Howells, and Jane Addams.

A year after the birth of the NAACP, the National Urban League was launched to deal with the problems created by the expanding black ghettos of the North. In the 1910-1920 decade a half-million Negroes had moved North to seek employment in industry and escape Southern oppression. In the North they found a more subtle discrimination that was no less effective than the overt persecution they had left behind.

Throughout this period before America entered World War I, individual Negroes contributed to important aspects of American life. Surgeon Daniel H. Williams performed the first operation on the human heart; he went on to make Provident Hospital in Chicago America's first integrated hospital and to open nursing to Negro women. Paul Laurence Dunbar's poetry made him one of America's best-loved writers. Matthew A. Henson became the first man to stand atop the world in 1909 when he reached the North Pole shortly before his commander, Robert E. Peary. Negro cavalrymen played a decisive role in the famous charge up San Juan Hill during the Spanish-American War. But neither the compromise offered by Booker T. Washington nor these contributions melted the solid walls of segregation.

Bibliography

1. John Hope Franklin, *From Slavery to Freedom* (Knopf, New York, 1967). Chapters XXI, XXII, and XXIII present a survey of the Negro's efforts to advance during these trying years. Franklin's information on Negro education, self-help, and the role of the Negro churches and white philanthropic societies is very interesting. Franklin devotes a chapter to the rise of American imperialism which discusses both the foreign aspects of American racism and the domestic counterparts to our acquisition of a vast empire of colored people. His discussion of the ideological debate between the followers of Washington and DuBois is valuable, as is his coverage of urban problems, race riots, and lynchings. Useful for teachers and high school upperclassmen.

2. Rayford W. Logan, *The Betrayal of the Negro* (Collier, New York, 1965, paperback), is a thorough examination of the Negro position in American society during this "nadir." The noted

Negro historian discusses discriminaton in the North and South, the leadership of Booker T. Washington, and the role of the Supreme Court in delineating the Negro's position in society. The Negro's crushing economic problems in industry and agriculture are carefully sketched. Useful for teachers and for research by high school students.

3. C. Vann Woodward, *The Strange Career of Jim Crow* (Oxford University Press, New York, 1957, and Galaxy paperback), demonstrates how and why the Jim Crow laws came during the post-Reconstruction period rather than earlier. Fascinating reading for teachers and high school students doing research.

4. William Loren Katz, *Eyewitness: The Negro in American History* (Pitman, New York, 1967, and paperback). Chapters 14 and 15 in text, pictures, and eyewitness accounts present the black struggle against discrimination during the "progressive era." For teachers and students.

5. W. E. B. DuBois, *The Souls of Black Folk* (Crest, New York, 1964, paperback). Chapter III is his famous answer to Booker T. Washington. Other chapters focus on the Negro's role in agriculture and industry. Useful for teachers and high school upperclassmen.

6. Francis L. Broderick and August Meier, eds., *Negro Protest Thought in the Twentieth Century* (Bobbs-Merrill, Indianapolis, 1965). Part I has documents of protest from 1895 to 1916, including the key arguments of Booker T. Washington and W. E. B. DuBois. The introductions set the stage for each entry. Useful for teachers and high school students.

7. Hugh Hawkins, *Booker T. Washington and His Critics: The Problem of Negro Leadership* (Heath, Boston, 1962, paperback), is a volume in the Amherst series of documentary studies of problems in American civilization. In the words of both contemporaries and noted historians, the volume presents the conflict over Booker T. Washington's views. Highly recommended for teachers and high school upperclassmen.

8. August Meier, *Negro Thought in America, 1880-1915: Racial Ideologies in the Age of Booker T. Washington* (University of Michigan Press, Ann Arbor, 1963, and paperback), is a

Dr. W. E. B. DuBois's Niagara Movement led to the formation of the NAACP. "The problem of the twentieth century," DuBois wrote in 1903, "is the problem of the color line."
Scurlock Studios

scholarly study of thought during this time of Booker T. Washington's leadership. Part Three is an excellent presentation of Washington's educational and political views, and Part Five discusses the radical and conservative crosscurrents in Negro thought. Chapter V establishes the continuing Negro militancy during this period of maximum oppression. Recommended for teachers and high school upperclassmen doing research.

9. Charles Flint Kellogg, *NAACP* (Johns Hopkins Press, Baltimore, 1967), is the scholarly story of the NAACP's first decade of struggle against racism. For teachers.

10. Dorothy Sterling and Benjamin Quarles, *Lift Every Voice* (Doubleday, New York, 1965, and paperback), is a series of four biographies: W. E. B. DuBois, Mary Church Terrell (reformer), Booker T. Washington, and James Weldon Johnson (diplomat, reformer, poet). This volume includes pictures of the four and is an excellent biographical study of Negro reformers of the period. It could be used effectively as a supplementary reader for junior high students.

11. Gilbert Osofsky, *The Burden of Race* (Harper & Row, New York, 1967, and paperback), contains many documents on this era of unbridled anti-Negro hate. Chapter V describes disfranchisement efforts, violence, anti-Negro literature, and stereotyped thinking. Chapter VI documents the voices of protest from the black community and the beginnings of important civil rights organizations in the North and South. This excellent source book for students' or teachers' research should also be used in class as supplementary reading.

12. Folkway Records, *W. E. B. DuBois: A Recorded Autobiography* (New York, 1961). Side I is the interesting story of the man whose Niagara Movement became the basis of the NAACP. Dr. DuBois' recording of his life story is interesting for its information and humor as well as its presentation of a rich life during an age of anti-Negro repression. Side I concludes with World War I. This is a useful classroom tool in secondary schools, but teachers should preview it first to determine portions they wish to stress or omit, and key phrases they want to define. The record package includes a copy of the complete text.

13. The McGraw-Hill filmstrips *The Negro in the Gilded Age* and *The Negro Faces the Twentieth Century* cover a wide variety of topics relating to the Negro during these periods. The former brings the Negro's story up to the Spanish-American War, and the first twenty frames of the latter take it up to the outbreak of World War I. Since these strips cover a wide range of topics briefly, the teacher should be prepared to present additional information to augment the subtitles. Recommended for students at any level.

14. Russell L. Adams, *Great Negroes Past and Present* (Afro-American, Chicago, 1964), includes biographies of Charles W. Chesnutt (novelist), Paul Laurence Dunbar (poet), W. E. B. DuBois, Colonel Charles Young (highest ranking Negro in U.S. Army), John Hope (educator), Daniel Hale Williams (surgeon), Dr. Ernest Just (biologist), Mary Church Terrell, Ebenezer Bassett (diplomat), John Mercer Langston (spokesman and diplomat), and William Monroe Trotter (editor). Useful for teachers and students doing research.

15. Milton Meltzer, ed., *In Their Own Words: A History of the American Negro, 1865-1916* (Crowell, New York, 1964, and paperback), includes documents by Negro anti-lynching reformers of this period. Each is preceded by an informative introduction. The use of pictures and the special editing of these accounts make them useful for high school students.

16. Langston Hughes, *Famous Negro Heroes of America* (Dodd, Mead, New York, 1958), has chapters on explorer Matt Henson, crusader Ida B. Wells, and Colonel Charles Young. Pictures and text are directed toward junior high readers.

17. Booker T. Washington, *Up from Slavery* (New York, many paperback editions), is the famous reformer's story of his successful campaigns to raise himself and increase his people's education. This autobiography is a particularly effective vehicle for presenting various aspects of the Negro's life and attitudes. Recommended highly for teachers and all students as outside reading.

18. Helen Buckler, *Daniel Hale Williams: Negro Surgeon* (Pitman, New York, 1968), is the biography of Daniel Hale Williams, who made medical history through his 1893 operation on the

human heart and then devoted his life to combating Jim Crow in the medical profession. It is a carefully researched and well-written biography that should be enjoyed by secondary school students.

19. Saunders Redding, *The Lonesome Road* (Doubleday, New York, 1958). Chapter V vividly describes the Negro troopers in the Spanish-American War; Chapter VI is the exciting story of Dr. Daniel Hale Williams. Because of his focus on prominent personalities to illustrate larger aspects of history, this writer's work should have special appeal for secondary school students.

20. Bradley Robinson, *Dark Companion* (McBride, New York, 1947, and Fawcett paperback), tells the authentic story of Matt Henson, the Negro explorer who became the first man to stand atop the world. Recommended for teachers and students, as it is the most accurate of several studies of Henson.

21. Carol F. Drisko and Edgar A. Toppin, *The Unfinished March* (Doubleday, New York, 1967, and paperback). Chapters 5 to 10 cover Negro activities during this era of lynch law, reform, and migration to the North. Chapter 5, particularly, is a superb exposition of America's assumption of the "White Man's Burden" at home and abroad at the turn of the century. Written for junior high school students and highly recommended as a supplementary text for this period of history.

22. *The Negro Problem, 1903* (Arno Press, New York, 1969, and paperback) is a reprint that presents the classic positions of Booker T. Washington and W. E. B. DuBois on black progress and includes other important black poets and novelists of the time. For research by teachers and senior high school students.

23. Ida Wells-Barnett, *On Lynchings* (Arno Press, New York, 1969, and paperback), reprints three pamphlets that attack lynchings. Research material for teachers and senior high school students.

24. Sutton Griggs, *Imperium in Imperio* (Arno Press, New York, 1969, and paperback), is a reprinted novel, by a black author, which depicts a black takeover of Texas. For outside reading.

25. W. E. B. DuBois, *The Philadelphia Negro: A Social Study* (Schocken Books, New York, 1967, and paperback), is a reprint

of Dr. DuBois's incisive sociological study and includes a new introduction. Highly recommended for teachers and high school upperclassmen doing research.

26. Edwin S. Redkey, *Black Exodus: Black Nationalist and Back-to-Africa Movements, 1890-1910* (Yale University Press, New Haven, 1969, and paperback), is an important study of Bishop Henry M. Turner and his pre-Garvey Back-to-Africa movement. Recommended for teachers and high school upperclassmen.

World War I and the Prosperity Decade

Dates to Remember

1917 Fifteen thousand New York Negroes march in a Silent Parade to protest the mounting number of lynchings and riots.

1919 W. E. B. DuBois organizes a Pan-African Congress in Paris.

1919 Twenty-five race riots erupt throughout the nation.

1925 A reinvigorated Ku Klux Klan marches forty thousand strong in front of the White House.

1925 Dr. Ossian Sweet of Detroit successfully defends his home, in a white neighborhood, against hoodlums.

1929 Oscar DePriest of Chicago becomes the first Northern Negro elected to Congress, and the first of his race since 1901.

At the outbreak of the First World War, American Negroes volunteered to serve their country. One hundred thousand were sent to France, more than forty thousand as combat troops. Most Negro units were assigned to French command, and the first two American winners of the coveted *Croix de Guerre,* Henry Johnson and Needham Roberts, were New York Negroes who wiped out a twenty-man German raiding party. Other entire Negro units won *Croix de Guerre* citations. The returning Negro veterans who marched up Fifth Avenue during the victory celebrations looked forward to enjoying at home some of the democracy they had fought to save abroad.

Before the parades had ended, Negroes had been lynched, some while still in U.S. Army uniforms. During the era of isolationism, disillusionment, and bigotry that followed the war, Negroes were able to make little headway toward equality. A revived Ku Klux Klan grew to five million members and broadened its hate program to include radicals, Catholics, Jews, foreigners, unionists, and liberals, as well as Negroes. By 1922 the NAACP drive for a federal anti-lynching bill met defeat when Southern Senators filibustered it to death.

The 1920's were also an age of radicalism. During the "Red Scare," A. Philip Randolph edited *The Messenger,* a radical-Socialist newspaper, that drew the attention of the Justice Department. Even the NAACP magazine, *The Crisis,* edited by W. E. B. DuBois, was visited by agents of the government investigating subversion. But the most powerful Negro leader in this age of radical movements was a short, pudgy Jamaican named Marcus Garvey. Intensely proud of his black color, he launched a crusade to unite Negroes behind a Back-to-Africa program. Although his campaign attracted millions, no one, not even Garvey, who had appointed himself Provisional President of Africa, left America.

Garvey's great appeal had been to urban Negroes, thousands of whom had poured into Northern and Southern ghettos to take war jobs. Throughout urban centers whites reacted with fear and loathing toward the new arrivals. Racial tensions also rose in middle-class neighborhoods as prosperious Negroes tried to move in. In 1925 a Detroit white mob attacked the home of Dr. Ossian Sweet and his family, but were driven off by gunfire. Charged with murder (one intruder had been killed), the Sweets were defended by the NAACP, which hired attorney Clarence Darrow. They won acquittal after Darrow proved the Negroes had done what all Americans had a right to do—defend their home. By 1929 Chicago Negroes were fighting for job rights by boycotting stores that did not hire Negro sales personnel—and winning victories in this field.

In the field of politics the Northern Negro demonstrated his voting strength in several places. In 1929 Oscar DePriest of Chicago became the first Negro elected to Congress from the North. A year later an NAACP campaign successfully defeated the Supreme Court nomination of a Judge Parker, who had expressed anti-Negro views.

But it was in the cultural area that the postwar Negro made his most significant contributions. Jazz, the music that gave the age its name, was brought from New Orleans to the North and to the world by black musicians. Harlem became the center of a vast cultural renaissance that attracted both the attention and support of wealthy whites. It was the home of poets Claude McKay, Countee Cullen, and Langston Hughes, the place to hear Duke Ellington's fabulous band and see popular Negro entertainers. Even Broadway featured Negro musicals and hired Negro soloists and actors in other productions. In this decade of prosperity, Negro talents often found white backers.

But the stock market crash brought everyone down a peg or two, and, as Langston Hughes noted, Negroes had few pegs to travel. The white backers disappeared from Harlem, and Negro talent joined white talent—on the breadlines. The Prosperity Decade, the Jazz Age, the Harlem Renaissance, all had ended together.

Bibliography

1. John Hope Franklin, *From Slavery to Freedom* (Knopf, New York, 1967). Chapters XXIV-XXVI present a rounded picture of Negro efforts in World War I, Negro resistance to growing postwar intolerance, and the Harlem Renaissance of the 1920's. Major cultural figures and works are examined. Recommended for teachers and high school students doing research.

2. Arna Bontemps and Jack Conroy, *Anyplace But Here* (Hill and Wang, New York, 1966, and paperback), has several chapters and sections devoted to figures of importance in this time period. Chapters XI and XII tell of Negro mass migrations to Chicago and the 1919 Chicago race riot. Vivid firsthand accounts by participants consistently enliven this readable volume. Chapter XIII is the story of Marcus Garvey and his Black Nationalist movement of the 1920's. Other sections describe the colorful jazz personalities W. C. Handy, Scott Joplin, and Jelly Roll Morton. This well-written and carefully researched volume will be valuable to teachers and high school students.

3. Langston Hughes, *The Big Sea* (Hill and Wang, New York, 1963, and paperback), is the autobiography of a poet, writer,

In July 1917, fifteen thousand New York Negroes protested the rise in lynchings and anti-Negro riots in a dramatic "Silent Parade," marching under NAACP sponsorship to the beat of muffled drums. *NAACP*

reporter, playwright, biographer, and historian. The third section presents his valuable personal impressions of the Harlem Renaissance. Through careful description and subtle humor, Hughes succeeds in making this epoch come to life. Recommended for teachers and high school students.

4. Francis L. Broderick and August Meier, *Negro Protest Thought in the Twentieth Century* (Bobbs-Merrill, Indianapolis, 1965). Section II includes writing by A. Philip Randolph, Langston . Hughes, R. Russa Moton (educator), E. Franklin Frazier (sociologist), and Marcus Garvey. The introductions to the readings provide valuable information. Recommended for teachers and high school students.

5. Gilbert Osofsky, *Harlem: The Making of a Ghetto* (Harper & Row, New York, 1966), describes the historical development of the Harlem community from its beginnings in the 1890's to its completion as a ghetto in the 1920's. Part Three studies the early development of Harlem's slums. Useful for teachers and high school students.

6. Langston Hughes, *Famous Negro Heroes of America* (Dodd, Mead, New York, 1954), includes chapters on Colonel Charles Young and World War I hero Private Henry Johnson. These short biographies are written for junior high readers.

7. Sterling A. Brown, Arthur P. Davis, and Ulysses Lee, eds., *The Negro Caravan* (Citadel, New York, 1941). Includes the writings of many Negroes who rose to fame during the 1920's or as a result of the Harlem Renaissance. For teachers wishing to integrate cultural contributions by drawing upon poetry, stories, and songs, this is the prime source. Highly recommended for teachers and high school students doing research.

8. Arna Bontemps, ed., *American Negro Poetry* (Hill and Wang, New York, 1966, and paperback), is a more limited selection of Negro poetic works. It includes a biography of each contributor. Recommended for teachers and students.

9. Russell L. Adams, *Great Negroes Past and Present* (Afro-American, Chicago, 1694), has biographical summaries and pictures of many Negroes of this period—scholars Alain L. Locke, Carter G. Woodson, Charles S. Johnson, and Mordecai Johnson;

leaders Marcus Garvey, Congressman DePriest, A. Philip Randolph, and Walter White (who investigated lynchings for the NAACP); publishers Robert S. Abbott and Robert L. Vann; and many figures from the fields of literature, entertainment, and religion. Recommended for teachers and students doing research.

10. Langston Hughes and Milton Meltzer, *A Pictorial History of the Negro in America* (Crown, New York, 1968). Pages 258-279 present pictures of Negroes prominent during this time in war, interracial organizations, the Harlem Renaissance, and the resistance to Jim Crow. Text and pictures are most useful for teachers and students.

11. The McGraw-Hill filmstrip *The Negro Faces the Twentieth-Century* includes an interesting picture history of the Negro from World War I to the election of Franklin D. Roosevelt in 1932. It covers the main political and cultural figures of the period. Careful teacher preparation of additional information can make this strip even more meaningful for students at any level.

12. Saunders Redding, *The Lonesome Road* (Doubleday, New York, 1958). Chapters VIII and IX are devoted to important Negro figures of the period from 1917 to 1939—Negro heroes of World War I, Marcus Garvey, A. Philip Randolph, Paul Robeson. This well-written narrative should be useful for high school students and teachers.

13. Milton Meltzer and August Meier, *Time of Trial, Time of Hope: The Negro in America, 1919-1941* (Doubleday, New York, 1966, and paperback), Chapters III to VII. Takes the story of the Negro from the First World War through the twenties, focusing on Negro urban and cultural movements. It includes pictures and is directed toward junior high readers.

14. Margaret Just Butcher, *The Negro in American Culture* (Knopf, New York, 1956, and paperback), is a thorough discussion and evaluation of Negro contributions to American music, poetry, polemics, fiction, drama, and art. This volume should be most helpful for teachers preparing a unit on American culture or for those who wish to stress Negro cultural advances during the 1920's.

15. Frederick Ramsey, Jr., and Charles Edward Smith, eds., *Jazzmen* (Harcourt Brace, New York, 1939, and paperback), is the story of the early jazz greats told by authorities in the field, often using eyewitness descriptions and superb photographs. Recommended for teachers and high school students.

16. William Loren Katz, *Eyewitness: The Negro in American History* (Pitman, New York, 1967, and paperback). Through text, pictures, and eyewitness accounts, Chapters 15 and 16 deal with black participation in World War I and with the period of the 1920's. It points up Negro resistance to Woodrow Wilson and the mounting discrimination against blacks. For teachers' research and students' supplementary reading.

17. Roi Ottley, *The Lonely Warrior: The Life and Times of Robert S. Abbott* (Regnery, Chicago, 1955), is a biography of the militant Negro editor of the *Chicago Defender*. Abbott is best known for his efforts to encourage Negro migration to the North during the First World War. Useful for teachers and high school students.

18. Alain Locke, ed., *The New Negro* (Arno Press, New York, and Atheneum, New York, 1968, paperback), is the reprint of a fine collection of black contributions to our culture during the Negro renaissance. Recommended for teachers and high school students as outside reading.

19. Peter Gammond, *Duke Ellington: His Life and Work* (Roy, New York, 1958), is the story of the famed jazz composer whose original contribution to the jazz of the twenties and our own time will always be remembered. It is told in essays by fourteen jazz authorities. Recommended for high school students doing research.

20. Amy-Jacques Garvey, ed., *Philosophy and Opinions of Marcus Garvey* (Arno Press, New York, 1968, paperback, and Atheneum, New York, 1969, paperback), reprints a double volume of the famous black separatist's basic ideas. Recommended for teachers and students doing research on this period.

21. Arthur I. Waskow, *From Race Riot to Sit-In* (Doubleday, New York, 1966, and paperback). Chapters II to X cover

the anti-Negro riots after World War I. Useful for students doing research.

22. Gordon Parks, *The Learning Tree* (Harper & Row, New York, 1963), is the story of a Negro family in Kansas during the 1920's. Because the focus is on young people living in the Middle West, this book has been successfully used as outside reading in junior and senior high classes. Highly recommended for all students.

23. *The Negro in Chicago: A Study of Race Relations and a Race Riot* (Arno Press, New York, 1968), is a reprinted classic about blacks in Chicago and the famous 1919 race riot. This volume contains basic material on black urban developments, the pattern of "ghettoization," and the exclusion of blacks from unions. For research by teachers and high school students.

24. Harold F. Gosnell, *Negro Politicians* (University of Chicago Press, Chicago, 1967, and paperback), is a study of political and racial relations in Chicago during the first few decades of the twentieth century. Chapter IX describes the rise of Oscar DePriest to Congress; Chapter XV describes Communist influence in the Negro ghetto during the early years of the Depression. Recommended for research by high school seniors.

25. E. David Cronon, *Black Moses* (University of Wisconsin Press, Madison, 1955, and paperback), is the story of Marcus Garvey and his campaigns in the Negro urban communities of America. Useful for research for high school students.

26. Emmett J. Scott, *The American Negro in the World War* (Arno Press, New York, 1969), reprints the best history of Negro participation in World War I. Documents and many photographs make the book a valuable research resource for students.

27. Emmett J. Scott, *Negro Migration During the War* (Arno Press, New York, 1969, and paperback), another reprint, is the best available history of the great migration that expanded the huge black ghettos of urban industrial centers. For research by teachers and high school students.

28. Walter White, *Rope and Faggot* (Arno Press, New York, 1969, and paperback), reprints the noted NAACP investigator's

report of lynchings and race riots in America after World War I. Good outside reading for teachers or high school students.

29. Rudolph Fisher, *The Walls of Jericho* (Arno Press, New York, 1969), a reprint, is a comic novel about the Harlem Renaissance. For outside reading by teachers or students.

Depression and the New Deal

Dates to Remember

1931 America and the world follow the famous Scottsboro Trial of nine Negro youths framed in Alabama.

1933 President Roosevelt hires many Negro advisers who form a "Black Cabinet."

1934 Arthur Mitchell, first Negro Democratic congressman, elected from Chicago; still one black in Congress.

1937 Joe Louis, Detroit's Brown Bomber, wins heavyweight crown from Braddock.

1937 William Hastie becomes first Negro federal judge.

1939 Marian Anderson, denied a Washington auditorium, sings before 75,000 at the Lincoln Memorial.

1941 A threatened march on Washington by Negroes leads to the first federal Fair Employment Practices Commission.

The Depression that crippled the United States during the 1930's hit the Negro wage earner with particular severity. The Negro found he was the last hired and the first fired, and Negro unemployment percentages soared above those for whites. By 1935 one-sixth of those on relief were Negroes—who constituted only one-tenth of the total U.S. population. But in several places the drive for security united Negroes and whites for jobs and relief. Even in the South, biracial committees demanded work and relief.

The most famous case to arise out of the Depression was the Scottsboro Trial of nine Negro youths falsely accused of attacking two female hobos. After an aroused nation and world protested this injustice, the young men finally won their liberty.

The Depression also brought American Negroes solidly into the ranks of the Democratic party after a long allegiance to the party of Lincoln. Some Northern Negro ghetto districts voted seven-to-one for Roosevelt, and Negroes throughout the nation hoped for an intelligent approach to race relations from the New Deal. The new President and his wife Eleanor did not often disappoint them. The "alphabet soup" of New Deal agencies were encouraged to hire Negro advisers, and soon Ralph Bunche, Robert C. Weaver, and Mary McCleod Bethune, to name only the most prominent, were serving in a Black Cabinet. The Roosevelt administration also hired Negro typists, agronomists, scientists, economists, and tax experts. The city of Washington, while still rigidly segregated, was the home of this growing class of government workers.

Negroes were among the main beneficiaries of the recovery programs instituted by the New Deal. They worked for the Works Progress Administration (which also established theater and art workshops in Negro ghettos), the Civilian Conservation Corps, and the National Youth Administration. Under government pressure, wage differentials based on color were altered. The C.I.O., aided greatly by friendly government legislation such as the Wagner Act, opened its doors to Negroes working in mass production industries. Interracial locals grew in steel, auto, and rubber factories, and Negro organizers and union officials became part of the C.I.O.'s drive for unionization. In the Southern Tenant Farmers' Union, formed by Arkansas sharecroppers in 1934, Negroes and whites joined together against their landlords.

Throughout the Depression, Negroes battled for their rights, aided by whites more than ever before. To force the hiring of Negro salespeople in Northern cities, Negroes organized "Don't Buy Where You Can't Work" campaigns. A 1935 riot in Harlem led to the employment of many more Negroes in the stores of the black ghetto. The NAACP began its legal battle to desegregate schools. And in April 1939, Secretary of the Interior Harold Ickes offered singer Marian Anderson the Lincoln Memorial for a concert after the Daughters of the American Revolution had denied her their Constitution Hall. From a stage that included

Senators, Cabinet members, and Supreme Court Judges, Miss Anderson sang to 75,000 Americans.

By far the most portentous protest of this time was the 1941 march on Washington planned by A. Philip Randolph to demand the hiring of Negroes in the growing defense industry. A few days before the march was scheduled, Randolph won from a reluctant President Roosevelt the first executive order concerning Negroes since the Emancipation Proclamation. Executive Order 8802 banned discrimination in the hiring policies of companies under government contract; it also established an FEPC to hear charges of discrimination. The New Deal era had brought significant gains to the Negro masses.

Bibliography

1. John Hope Franklin, *From Slavery to Freedom* (Knopf, New York, 1967). Chapter XXVII presents the many benefits Negroes gave to and received from the New Deal. Among the important topics discussed are the Black Cabinet, relief measures, the rise in Negro government employment, and the battle against discrimination during this period of increased hope.

2. Roi Ottley, *New World A-Coming* (Houghton Mifflin, Boston, 1943). A famous Negro reporter's recollection of the New Deal period. It includes descriptions of Negro leaders, Harlem, Father Divine, Joe Louis, the Negro press, and the projected march on Washington. Besides his own interesting reminiscences, Ottley draws upon contemporary comments. Recommended for teachers and high school students.

3. Francis L. Broderick and August Meier, *Negro Protest Thought in the Twentieth Century* (Bobbs-Merrill, Indianapolis, 1965). Part III presents the words of the leading Negro spokesmen of this period and includes Negro reactions to communism's appeal during this time of national economic stress. Each document is preceded by an informative introduction. Recommended for teachers and high school students.

4. Langston Hughes, *I Wonder as I Wander* (Hill and Wang, New York, 1966, and paperback), is the famous writer's story of his adventures during the 1930's. His odyssey took him to

Communist Russia, the Spanish Civil War, the Orient, and America's Northern and Southern states. His delightful writing style and fascinating journeys make this a most interesting book for high school students. Recommended for high school students' outside reading or research.

5. Richard Bardolph, *The Negro Vanguard* (Holt, Rinehart & Winston, New York, 1959, and Vintage paperback), is a thorough and scholarly study of the backgrounds of America's Negro leadership class. Its information on Negroes of the New Deal period, found in Parts II and III, is particularly interesting. Bardolph's focus is on the familial, economic, and discriminatory backgrounds of Negro leaders rather than their accomplishments. Useful for research by high school upperclassmen.

6. Gilbert Osofsky, *The Burden of Race* (Harper & Row, New York, 1967), in Chapter VIII has some excellent documents on difficulties faced by black America during the New Deal. It includes material on the Scottsboro Case, the CIO, the March-on-Washington movement, and the New Deal era of FDR. Recommended for teachers' research and high school students' reading.

7. Marian Anderson, *My Lord, What a Morning* (Viking, New York, 1956, and Avon paperback), is the autobiography of the renowned Negro contralto. It describes her historic concert at the Lincoln Memorial in 1939, her trips to Europe, and her experiences on the concert stage and off. Recommended for secondary school students as either outside reading or research material.

8. William Loren Katz, *Eyewitness: The Negro in American History* (Pitman, New York, 1967, and paperback). Chapter XVII describes the Negro in the Depression, New Deal agencies, civil rights activities, and as part of the opposition to Nazi racism and aggression. Pictures and documents depict the Negro's part in the CCC, TVA, Congress, and the C.I.O. Recommended for teachers and students.

9. Catherine Owens Peare, *Mary McLeod Bethune* (Vanguard, New York, 1961), is the biography of the leading member of the Black Cabinet—the woman who, more than any other Negro, had the ear of President and Mrs. Roosevelt. Mrs. Bethune rose

Mrs. Mary McLeod Bethune, founder of a Florida college for Negro
women, became the leading member of President Franklin D.
Roosevelt's "Black Cabinet." New Deal efforts to overcome the
Great Depression convinced the vast majority of Negro voters to
support the Democratic party.
Harmon Foundation

from poverty to become a college president and, finally, adviser to Presidents Roosevelt and Truman. Recommended for secondary students as outside reading or for research.

10. Arna Bontemps, *Famous Negro Athletes* (Dodd, Mead, New York, 1964), has chapters devoted to Joe Louis and Jesse Owens. A crisp writing style makes these chapters interesting as well as informative for students. Recommended for secondary school students.

11. Richard Wright, *Uncle Tom's Children* (New American Library, New York, paperback), and *Native Son* (Signet, New York, paperback), are fictionalized accounts of the Negro's experience during the American Depression. The former is a collection of short stories depicting the Negro's violent life in the deep South; the latter is the story of a Chicago ghetto dweller who is crushed by society. Both books are powerful and provocative, historically interesting and informative, and provide an emotional depth that nonfiction cannot convey. Recommended for high school students as outside reading in English or social studies classes.

12. The McGraw-Hill filmstrip *The Negro Fights for the "Four Freedoms"* traces the Negro role in American history from the elections of 1934 to 1954. Its excellent color pictures illustrate Negro contributions to the New Deal and victory in World War II. Highly recommended for any class.

13. Langston Hughes and Milton Meltzer, *A Pictorial History of the Negro in America* (Crown, New York, 1968). Pages 280-291 cover New Deal events and personalities in pictures and text. A useful tool for class display, research, and general information. Teachers will find this section brief and clear, the pictures suitable for many purposes.

14. Rayford W. Logan and Irving S. Cohen, *The American Negro* (Houghton Mifflin, Boston, 1967, paperback). Chapter VIII provides information on the problems of blacks during the New Deal era as well as on their contributions. Recommended for supplementary reading by junior high school students.

15. Angelo Herndon, *Let Me Live* (Arno Press, New York, 1969, and paperback), reprints the autobiography of a black

Communist whose leadership of an integrated unemployment demonstration in Georgia during the Depression became a *cause célèbre*. Howard Meyer's new introduction sheds light on the cause and the time. Recommended for outside reading by teachers and high school upperclassmen.

16. Richard Wright, *12 Million Black Voices* (Arno Press, New York, 1969), a reprint, is a notable illustrated essay on black America during the Great Depression. The excellent text and photographs should make this volume useful for teachers and students doing outside reading or research.

17. Milton Meltzer and August Meier, *Time of Trial, Time of Hope* (Doubleday, New York, 1966, and paperback). Chapters VIII through XIII describe Negroes during the Depression and the New Deal, their role in the C.I.O., and the projected 1941 march on Washington. Recommended for junior high readers as a supplementary text.

World War II and After, 1941-1953

Dates to Remember

1941 Dr. Charles Drew develops the British blood bank system.

1941 Sailor Dorie Miller becomes first American hero of World War II by bringing down four Japanese planes at Pearl Harbor, but is denied the Medal of Honor.

1942 Congress of Racial Equality (CORE) formed by Negro and white believers in non-violent direct action against discrimination.

1943 Detroit's anti-Negro riot disrupts the U.S. war effort.

1945 New York becomes the first to pass a state FEPC.

1946 President Harry Truman appoints William Hastie Governor of the Virgin Islands.

1948 President Truman's Executive Order 9981 initiates desegregation of the armed forces.

1950 For his part in bringing peace to the Holy Land, Dr. Ralph Bunche is awarded the Nobel Peace Prize.

From the attack on Pearl Harbor until final victory over Japan, American Negroes were part of their country's massive World War II effort. Three million Negroes registered for Selective Service and half a million Negro men and women saw service overseas; most Negro units, however, were assigned menial work. Navy Pearl Harbor hero Dorie Miller was a messmate, the rating assigned to Negro sailors. Only in 1943 did the Marines break their 167-year tradition by accepting Negro applicants.

Negro units took part in naval, air, and land battles in both the European and Pacific theaters of war. They were Seabees, Marines, foot soldiers, tankmen, artillerymen, anti-aircraftmen, and engineers. They were among those who landed in North Africa, in Italy, and in France on D-Day. Negro airmen of the 99th and 332nd Pursuit Squadrons, trained in both integrated and segregated camps, made an enviable record in the skies over North Africa, Italy, France, and central Europe. But the only successful breakthrough in armed forces integration came during the famous Battle of the Bulge, when General Eisenhower's urgent call for volunteers from behind the lines resulted in thousands of Negro servicemen joining whites to drive back the Nazi thrust. After the battle, segregation was restored.

The war against fascism was not without its bitter behind-the-scenes battles to keep American racism. Detroit, a major production center for the U.S. war effort, had attracted thousands of Southern white and Negro migrants. In 1943 it saw four days of anti-Negro violence. NAACP troubleshooter Walter White toured battlefront and home-front centers of racial friction, including Guam, where brief warfare broke out between Negro and white troops.

World War II gave important impetus to those who sought the removal of Jim Crow restrictions. In 1942 CORE was formed to combat discrimination through direct action and the use of non-violence. Its "sit-ins" soon desegregrated Chicago restaurants and swimming pools and a New Jersey amusement park. In 1946 Americans welcomed the news that Jackie Robinson had broken baseball's color line, and the Negro veterans in Birmingham, Alabama, were marching to voter registration stations. President Truman's appointment of a Commission on Human Rights in 1946 and his armed forces desegregation order of 1948 were part of the campaign for equality and justice in America. Truman's 1948 election victory came despite defections from the right and left wings of his Democratic party, caused in part by his position on civil rights.

The birth of the United Nations and the Cold War provided additional momentum for civil rights crusaders. The UN's Declaration of Human Rights and the appointment of Negroes to the United States UN delegation encouraged Negro hopes for a better life in postwar America. Similarly, the rise of world communism increasingly made racial injustice in the United States a dangerous disadvantage in the Cold War. The racial issue was often brought home to the world by African UN delegates who were refused admittance to American restaurants and hotels. Some American Negroes found they could secure service in certain restaurants if they dressed as African diplomats.

A most significant factor in the movement to eliminate American racial injustice was the emergence of African nations from years of colonial rule. As each new nation joined the UN it became increasingly clear that two-thirds of the world's people were non-white. The arrival and demeanor of these delegates also added a new dimension to the growing pride of American Negroes. The State Department began to see the importance of solving America's racial injustices and appointing Negro ambassadors in a world that was largely non-white. Presidents Eisenhower, Kennedy, and Johnson appointed Negro ambassadors to white and non-white nations, and the State Department began a recruiting drive to enlist more Negroes in the foreign service.

Bibliography

1. John Hope Franklin, *From Slavery to Freedom* (Knopf, New York, 1967). Chapters XXIX and XXX discuss the Negro's role in World War II and his reasons for hope in the postwar world. These concluding chapters of Franklin's classic history of the American Negro reflect his own cautious optimism about the talk of freedom and justice resulting from World War II and the new United Nations. Recommended for teachers and high school students.

2. Francis L. Broderick and August Meier, eds., *Negro Protest Thought in the Twentieth Century* (Bobbs-Merrill, Indianapolis, 1965). Section III presents eight documents dealing with Negro strivings during this period. Recommended for teachers and high school students.

3. Saunders Redding, *The Lonesome Road* (Doubleday, New York, 1958). Chapters X and XI relate interesting stories of Negroes during the war and postwar periods. One tells of a successful attempt to integrate the U.S. Army during a World War II

Members of the Negro 93rd Division wade across a river on a South Pacific island during World War II. As in World War I, most Negro GI's were assigned to "service" rather than combat units.
U.S. Army

battle; the second is about Thurgood Marshall, the NAACP attorney who argued and won many civil rights cases before the Supreme Court. Both chapters are well written and should be useful to teachers and high school students.

4. Francis L. Broderick, *W. E. B. DuBois* (Stanford University Press, Stanford, 1959, and paperback), is the story of the brilliant Negro leader and writer. In this readable and useful biography, Broderick tries to explain Dubois's place in history and his interest in left-wing politics. Recommended for outside reading or research by high school upperclassmen.

5. *W. E. B. DuBois, A Recorded Autobiography* (Folkways, New York) is the story of the Negro leader told in his own interesting words. In Part II, DuBois describes Negro reactions to emerging African nations, the United Nations, communism, and other world problems. A useful classroom tool for high school students.

6. Rayford W. Logan, *The Negro in the United States* (Van Nostrand, Princeton, N.J., 1957, paperback). Chapter VI and Documents 15 through 21 tell the story of the Negro drive for equality in World War II and its aftermath. The documents include President Truman's executive order abolishing armed forces segregation and several Supreme Court decisions. Useful for teachers and high school students doing research on the legal aspects of the Negro's progress.

7. The McGraw-Hill filmstrip *The Negro Fights for the "Four Freedoms"* details the story of the Negro during this period of American history. Recommended for classroom presentation on any level.

8. William Loren Katz, *Eyewitness: The Negro in American History* (Pitman, New York, 1967). Chapter 18 depicts the part played by blacks in World War II and after. For teachers and students.

9. Carl T. Rowan with Jackie Robinson, *Wait Till Next Year* (Random House, New York, 1960), is the exciting story of the athlete who broke baseball's color ban. One of several biographies of the Dodgers star, this one is written for adults and should be useful for teachers and high school students as outside reading.

A. Philip Randolph, labor leader, who organized the 1941 March on Washington.
Harmon Foundation

10. Ethel Waters with Charles Samuels, *His Eye Is on the Sparrow* (Doubleday, New York, 1951, and paperback), is the autobiography of the famous actress and singer. Recommended for high school students as outside reading.

11. Richard Wright, *Black Boy* (World, Cleveland, 1945, and paperback), is the hard-hitting autobiographical novel of a Negro growing up in a Chicago ghetto. High school students will find that these incidents of discrimination and deprivation reinforce statistical data.

12. Harold R. Isaacs, *The New World of Negro Americans* (Viking, New York, 1963, and paperback), is a study of the impact of world affairs upon Negro Americans. The section on the Negro and his attitude toward African people and states is particularly valuable. Recommended for teachers.

13. J. Alvin Kugelmass, *Ralph J. Bunche, Fighter for Peace* (Messner, New York, 1952), is the biography of the Nobel Prize winner. Recommended for teachers or secondary students as outside reading.

14. Langston Hughes, *Famous Negro Heroes of America* (Dodd, Mead, New York, 1958), includes chapters on Hugh Mulzac (Negro Merchant Marine captain in World War II), Dorie Miller, and Benjamin O. Davis, Jr., of the Air Force. Recommended for junior high students.

15. John D. Silvera, *The Negro in World War II* (Arno Press, New York, 1969), is a reprint of the only picture history of blacks' participation in World War II. Easy reading. Recommended for students, either as supplementary reading or as research material.

16. Louise Jefferson, *Twentieth-Century Americans of Negro Lineage* (Friendship Press, New York, 1963), is a beautiful colored pictomap that illustrates the contributions to American life made by famous Negroes of our day. A useful teachers' guide comes with the map, which is suitable for display or framing. Friendship Press in New York also offers large pictures (8½ by 11 inches) of famous Negroes mentioned on the pictomap.

17. Homer Smith, *Black Man in Red Russia* (Johnson, Chicago, 1964), is the story of a Negro reporter's fourteen years

covering the Kremlin. Recommended for secondary students as outside reading.

18. Ulysses Lee, *The Employment of Negro Troops* (United States Army, Washington, D.C., 1966), is a massive volume describing the part Negro soldiers played in World War II. Its twenty-two chapters, many maps, tables, and pictures represent a gigantic effort to evaluate the difficulties and successes of Negro soldiers and airmen in the war against the Axis powers. Recommended for special research by interested high school upperclassmen.

19. Ralph Ellison, *Invisible Man* (Random House, New York, 1947, and Signet paperback), is a novel based on the author's experiences as a sensitive young Negro in a brutal white world. Particularly interesting is his account of his relationship to the Brotherhood—the Communist party. Highly recommended as outside reading for high school upperclassmen.

America's Civil Rights Crusade

Dates to Remember

1954 U.S. Supreme Court rules segregated schools inherently unequal, reversing a half-century of legal segregation.

1955 A Negro boycott of Montgomery, Alabama, buses is led to a successful conclusion by Dr. Martin Luther King, Jr.

1957 President Eisenhower orders federal troops into Little Rock, Arkansas, to enforce court-ordered school integration.

1960 Four North Carolina college students begin a lunch counter sit-in; the movement spreads south and north.

1961 Freedom Riders testing desegregation of interstate buses are mobbed in Birmingham, Alabama. Kennedy administration provides U.S. marshals for protection.

1962 James Meredith, guarded by U.S. marshals, becomes first Negro to enroll at University of Mississippi.

1963 Civil rights demonstrations reach a peak in North and South.

1963 More than 200,000 Americans march on Washington to demand civil rights legislation and jobs.

In 1954 the Supreme Court ruled unanimously that school segregation violated the United States Constitution. While many school districts in the upper South desegregated quietly, those in the deep South began a program of evasion or massive resistance. President Eisenhower ordered the desegregation of Washington, D.C., schools and facilities but never spoke in favor of the Supreme Court decision. But by 1957 he ordered federal troops into Arkansas when Governor Orval Faubus obstructed a court order to admit nine Negro pupils to Central High School in Little Rock.

Using tactics of non-violent resistance he had learned from studying Henry David Thoreau and Mahatma Gandhi, Rev. Martin Luther King, Jr., led Montgomery, Alabama, Negroes in an effective boycott of the city's segregated buses. Dr. King became the Negro leader of his day, his principle of non-violent resistance to unjust laws the theme of the growing civil rights movement.

A more forceful phase of the civil rights drive began in 1960 with the student sit-ins to desegregate Southern lunch counters. New civil rights groups such as the Student Non-violent Coordinating Committee (SNCC) were formed, and older organizations such as CORE, the Urban League, and the NAACP adopted the methods of direct actionists. In 1961 CORE launched the Freedom Ride movement to test desegregation of interstate travel facilities. When the demonstrators were assaulted in Birmingham, Alabama, President Kennedy ordered federal marshals to protect them on their trips. A reluctant federal government was being drawn into the struggle for civil rights.

The government gradually gave more support to the black demand for full American citizenship. Congress passed weak civil rights laws in 1957 and 1960 and stronger ones in 1964 and 1965. Since the New Deal the Supreme Court had increasingly ruled in favor of equal rights. Use of presidential power in matters of Negro rights had grown during and after the New Deal, particularly in the Kennedy and Johnson administrations. A significant factor in determining government action was the rising voting power of the Northern and Southern Negro ghettos: they helped to tip the election outcome to Kennedy in 1960 and supported Johnson by 95 per cent in 1964.

As the Negro marched toward full equality in the America of the 1960's, he was supported by an impressive and growing number of federal, state, and local laws. In 1957, 1960, 1964, and 1965, Congress passed legislation to protect school desegregation from interference and halt interference with Negro voters in the South. These laws extended the power of the U.S. Attorney General in civil rights cases, provided for the curtailment of federal funds to projects that did not eliminate discrimination, and forbade unions, businesses, and public accommodations to practice racial discrimination.

After World War II many states had moved to eliminate racial discrimination. In 1945 New York passed the first state Fair Employment Practices Act; twenty states have followed her lead. In 1959 Colorado passed a law prohibiting housing discrimination, and seven states have followed her example. Discrimination in the use of public recreation facilities has been banned by twenty-eight states. Until 1967, when the United States Supreme Court declared these laws unconstitutional, twenty-one states prohibited interracial marriages.

But despite all laws, presidential actions, and Supreme Court decisions, the order of the day was gradualism and tokenism. Besides, a massive white backlash movement was mounting, prepared to use every weapon, from votes to violence, to halt integration.

Bibliography

1. Anthony Lewis and the *New York Times, Portrait of a Decade: The Second American Revolution* (Random House, New York, 1964, and paperback), is a comprehensive account of the ten years following the 1954 Supreme Court decision. By quoting news stories and the words of participants in the Negro revolution of today, this book presents a vivid word picture of the main events. Highly recommended for teachers and high school students as a supplementary text.

2. Francis L. Broderick and August Meier, *Negro Protest Thought in the Twentieth Century* (Bobbs-Merrill, Indianapolis, 1965). Part IV has twenty documents by leaders of today's Negro revolution, including Martin Luther King, Jr., Whitney Young, Jr., Bayard Rustin, novelist John O. Killens, Malcolm X, Roy Wilkins, and James Farmer. Recommended for teachers and high school students doing research.

3. Martin Luther King, Jr., *Stride Toward Freedom* (Harper, New York, 1958, and Ballantine paperback), and *Why We Can't Wait* (Harper & Row, New York, 1964, and Signet paperback),

Dr. Martin Luther King, Jr., whose philosophy of non-violent resistance to the evils of discrimination earned him the Nobel Peace Prize
in 1964. He successfully led the 1956 Montgomery bus boycott and
helped organize the 1963 March on Washington.
Southern Christian Leadership Conference

are readable accounts of the civil rights revolution by its leader. The first book discusses the Montgomery bus boycott and the theory of non-violence that won Dr. King the Nobel Peace Prize; the second describes the civil rights crusade of the early 1960's and includes the famous "Letter from a Birmingham Jail." Both volumes are useful for teachers and high school students doing research.

4. Sammy Davis, Jr., *Yes I Can* (Farrar, Straus, New York, 1965, and Pocket Books paperback), is the moving story of the talented Negro entertainer. In clear prose and interesting photographs, Davis tells his rags-to-riches story. Recommended for teachers and all students.

5. James Peck, *Freedom Ride* (Simon & Schuster, New York, 1962, and Grove paperback), recounts the non-violent resistance of a white Freedom Rider who was almost beaten to death in Birmingham. Peck also tells of his earlier non-violent labors for CORE in the North. Recommended for teachers and high school students for outside reading or research.

6. John Howard Griffin, *Black like Me* (Harcourt Brace, New York, 1961, and Signet paperback), is the fascinating story of a white professor who dyed his skin so he could enter the South as a Negro. His experiences are frightening as well as entertaining. This book brings to life a good deal of information about discrimination. It is a highly effective teaching tool for high school students.

7. Charles E. Silberman, *Crisis in Black and White* (Random House, New York, 1964, and Vintage paperback), is a white reporter's honest evaluation of the many aspects of today's racial crisis. Recommended for teachers and high school upperclassmen as outside reading or research.

8. E. Frederick Morrow, *Black Man in the White House* (Coward-McCann, New York, 1963, and McFadden paperback), is the diary of America's first Negro presidential aide. The man who served President Eisenhower and then in Vice President Nixon's 1960 campaign provides some valuable insights into the political complexities and inequities of mid-century America. Recommended for teachers and high school students as outside reading or research.

9. Michael Harrington, *The Other America: Poverty in the United States* (Macmillan, New York, 1962, and Penguin paperback). Chapter IV discusses Negro poverty and life in American urban ghettos. In interesting, readable prose and a few but potent statistics, Harrington conveys a picture of what it means to be black and poor in America. Highly recommended for teachers and high school students.

10. Doris E. Saunders, *The Day They Marched* (Johnson, Chicago, 1963, paperback), and *The Kennedy Years and the Negro* (Johnson, Chicago, 1964), feature photographs of historic events during the Kennedy administration. The first is a pictorial study of the March on Washington, and the second is a history of the Kennedy administration's relation to the mounting racial crisis. Both should be useful in any class.

11. Naomi and Arnold Buchheimer, *Equality Through Integration* (Anti-Defamation League, New York, 1965, paperback), is the success story of a New York State district that integrated its schools years before the 1954 Supreme Court decision and has been profiting ever since. Interesting reading and pictures. Recommended for all teachers and students.

12. Langston Hughes, *Fight for Freedom* (Norton, New York, 1962, paperback). Chapters 5 and 6 take the civil rights story from the 1954 decision to 1962. This fast-moving summary should be useful for teachers and high school students.

13. Elizabeth Sutherland, ed., *Letters from Mississippi* (McGraw-Hill, New York, 1965, and Signet paperback), is the story of the 1964 Mississippi project told in the words of the young people who went south to teach or assist in voter registration. This interesting collection of letters should be of value to teachers and all students wishing to understand what it meant to live in the South and help Mississippi Negroes attain their rights in the 1960's.

14. Howard Zinn, *SNCC: The New Abolitionists* (Beacon, Boston, 1966, paperback), is a short history of the radical Student Non-violent Coordinating Committee by an admiring historian. Zinn makes use of many quotations to implement his realistic story. Recommended for teachers and high school students as outside reading or research.

15. Langston Hughes and Milton Meltzer, *A Pictorial History of the Negro in America* (Crown, New York, 1964). Pages 304-334 summarize the major events in the civil rights crisis through photographs and text. Recommended for teachers and all students.

16. Gordon W. Allport, *The Nature of Prejudice* (Addison-Wesley, New York, 1954, and Anchor paperback), is the classic study of the causes and cures of prejudice. Useful for teachers and high school upperclassmen doing research on the nature of anti-Negro prejudice.

17. The following movies, useful in high school classes, are available from the offices of the Anti-Defamation League, New York City:

A Morning for Jimmy, 28 minutes, black and white; story of job discrimination against a Negro boy and how he and his teacher help overcome it.

All the Way Home, 29½ minutes, black and white; white reactions to Negroes moving into their neighborhood and how responsible community leadership can successfully integrate communities.

Crisis in Levittown, 31½ minutes, black and white; discusses the problem of equality of opportunity in housing through interviews with residents of a Pennsylvania community that is to be integrated.

No Hiding Place, 50 minutes, black and white; traces the difficulties of a Negro family that has just moved into a white neighborhood. From the television series "East Side, West Side," featuring George C. Scott.

Report from Atlanta, 29½ minutes, black and white; telecast of Civil Rights Commission hearings on voting rights in Montgomery, Alabama.

Walk in My Shoes, 42 minutes, black and white; powerful documentary on how the Negro reacts to prejudice; told through the words of many Negroes.

Dallas at the Crossroads, 28 minutes, black and white; in describing the desegregation of Dallas public schools, the film indicates how this can be accomplished peacefully.

The Other Face of Dixie, 53 minutes, black and white; the story of progress in Southern desegregation told in the words of the students and teachers who helped bring it about.

18. Lorenz Graham, *South Town* (Follett, Chicago, 1960, and Signet paperback), and *North Town* (Crowell, New York, 1965, and paperback), are interesting fictionalized novels of prejudice told for junior high readers.

19. Dorothy Sterling, *Mary Jane* (Doubleday, New York, 1959, and paperback), is the story of a young student who integrates a Southern junior high school. Highly recommended for junior high students.

20. *Reports of the President's Commission on Civil Rights* (Government Printing Office, Washington, D.C.). These reports are issued each year and often contain valuable information about civil rights developments and discrimination. They may be obtained from the Commission's offices in Washington, D.C.

21. The *New York Times* filmstrip (black and white) *Integration's Ten-Year March* tells of efforts to integrate American schools during the ten years since the 1954 Supreme Court decision. It is based on photographs of the outstanding civil rights events of our day. Useful for class introduction or summary of the struggle for equal rights.

22. Sally Belfrage, *Freedom Summer* (Viking, New York, 1965, and paperback), is the story of a young white volunteer in the 1964 Mississippi Summer Project. A tersely written and exciting account of the commitment of young freedom workers and the bravery of Mississippi Negroes. Hanging over this fateful summer was the disappearance and murder of three young civil rights workers. Recommended for teachers and students as outside reading.

23. Lorraine Hansberry, *The Movement* (Simon & Schuster, New York, 1964, paperback), is a pictorial history of the struggle for equality during the last ten years, based upon action photographs and a text written by the famous Negro playwright. Recommended for students and teachers.

24. Althea Gibson, *I Always Wanted to Be Somebody* (Harper, New York, 1958, and paperback), is the biography of the Negro tennis star who rose from the squalor of Harlem streets to world fame. A highly interesting and readable story for students interested in sports.

25. John Williams, ed., *The Angry Black* (Lancer, New York, 1962, paperback), is composed of twelve stories and articles by writers expressing the angry mood of those facing discrimination. Among the contributors are James Baldwin, Ralph Ellison, Richard Wright, and editor John Williams.

26. Guy and Candie Carawan, eds., *We Shall Overcome!* (Oak, New York, 1963, paperback), is a compilation of the songs of the Southern Freedom Movement. It includes music and lyrics, pictures, and many accounts by participants. It could be used in music classes as well as social studies courses. Recommended for all students interested in the music that grew out of the civil rights movement in the South.

27. Gilbert Osofsky, *The Burden of Race* (Harper & Row, New York, 1967), is a documentary history of race relations in America since Colonial times. The more than one hundred pages of text and documents in the last chapter provide many interesting and vivid examples of civil rights activities and the viewpoints of white segregationists and black-power advocates. Recommended for teachers and for high school students doing research.

28. John Hope Franklin, *From Slavery to Freedom* (Knopf, New York, 1967, and paperback). Chapter 31 discusses civil rights revolution in the author's typical thorough fashion. Recommended for research by teachers and senior high school students.

29. Rayford W. Logan and Irving S. Cohen, *The American Negro* (Houghton Mifflin, Boston, 1967). Chapter 9, devoted to the civil rights movement, is typical textbook pedantry. For research by junior high school students.

30. Richard C. Wade, *The Negro in American Life* (Houghton Mifflin, Boston, 1965). Chapter 8 presents seven documents having to do with the civil rights movement. For high school students' research.

31. William Loren Katz, *Eyewitness: The Negro in American History* (Pitman, New York, 1967, and paperback). Chapter 19 tells the story of the civil rights revolution, using pictures and eyewitness accounts to illuminate the text. For reading and research by both teachers and students.

32. Joanne Grant, *Black Protest* (Fawcett, New York, 1968, paperback). Part VI includes many important documents on the civil rights revolution. A vital source for research by teachers and students.

33. Henry Steele Commager, ed., *The Struggle for Racial Equality* (Harper & Row, New York, 1967, paperback). Documents 12 through 34 depict the civil-rights-movement decade. For research by teachers and senior high school students.

34. I. A. Newby, *Challenge to the Court* (Louisiana State University Press, Baton Rouge, 1969), dissects, through social science, those who have assailed the notion of equality. For research by teachers.

The Black Revolution

Dates to Remember

1964 Demonstrations in New York City escalate the "white backlash."

1965 The Meredith March leads to the "Black Power" slogan.

1967 Thurgood Marshall is appointed to the U.S. Supreme Court.

1968 The assassination of Dr. Martin Luther King, Jr., ends an era of black non-violence.

1968 The Poor People's March on Washington unites many minorities.

1969 Armed black students at Cornell shock a nation.

1970 The Nixon administration initiates a period of "benign neglect" of black America, cutting back funds for ghettos.

While the 1963 March on Washington marked the high point of the civil rights crusade, black Americans in the years immediately following were filled with disappointment and resentment. The Kerner Commission report, issued after the 1967 ghetto uprisings in Newark and Detroit, found the nation "moving toward two societies, one black, one white—separate and unequal." This perceptive document, which revealed a deep sensitivity toward black citizens, pinpointed traditional American racism as the root cause of riots and refused to accept the prevalent myth that white Communists or black extremists were responsible for mass violence. But neither President Johnson, who authorized the Kerner Commission, nor President Nixon, who followed him, endorsed its findings.

The attitude of white Americans toward blacks had not really changed after a decade of civil rights activities. They still failed to appreciate the plight of black citizens. The "white backlash," as it came to be called, escalated as soon as Northern blacks demanded the removal of invisible bars blocking advancement. In 1964 New York City parents mounted huge anti-integration demonstrations against the schools. Three times in 1968, New York teachers struck against the school system to prevent community control of ghetto schools. In Chicago, during a demonstration for open housing in 1966, Dr. Martin Luther King, Jr., noted, "I have seen many demonstrations in the South, but I have never seen any so hostile and so hateful as I have seen here today."

The ghetto riots and rebellions that began in 1964 and reached their peak in 1968 were born of utter desperation. Black ghettos had been unaffected by civil rights laws and were hardly touched by the administration's war on poverty. Ghetto schools, transportation, public services, recreational facilities, and job opportunities lagged far behind those in white communities. When rioters took to the streets to mark their desperation, local police, supported by National Guard troops, used force to suppress the rebelliousness. Almost all the people who died or were injured were black. Yet the white communities asked for more police control in the ghettos and repeatedly voted for "law and order" candidates. Most chose to ignore the Kerner Commission's finding that the rioters were *not* unemployed newcomers from the South on a wild spree, but young, informed blacks who were determined to do something about ghetto conditions.

Militancy rose in the black communities throughout the 1960's. In most civil rights organizations white and older black leaders were replaced by outspoken young blacks. In CORE and SNCC white members were rejected, and the goal of integration was abandoned in favor of "community control." Non-violence was no longer considered the best response to the white blacklash. These black organizations, beginning with SNCC in 1965, denounced the war in Vietnam as imperialist aggression against a non-white and colonial people. Soon all the black organizations except the NAACP opposed the Vietnam war. In 1967 Dr. Martin Luther King, Jr., and Stokely Carmichael of SNCC led a giant march in New York City to protest the war and the draft. By 1970, 9 per cent of the black population considered themselves "revolutionaries," and 40 per cent of the young blacks thought violence might well be necessary to achieve racial equality.

New black movements and leaders arose to meet the demands of this new militancy. On college campuses, black students grouped together to press for Afro-American studies and often for separate dormitories and recreational facilities as well. At Cornell in 1969 the nation reacted with shock when armed black students won concessions from a confused white college administration. The Black Panther party rejected black separatism, but its members armed for self-defense and fought several battles with police "pigs." Their outstanding spokesman, Eldridge Cleaver, wrote *Soul on Ice,* which became, along with Malcolm X's autobiography, a bible for young blacks. Police persecution decimated the Panther ranks and drove Cleaver from the country. Other leaders of young blacks included Stokely Carmichael, whose "Black Power" slogan was interpreted by whites to mean the burning of cities; H. Rap Brown, an outspoken advocate of violence who maintained that "violence is as American as apple pie"; LeRoi Jones, a black poet whose many books of verse, plays, and essays were popular among black readers; and Julius Lester, a social critic, whose writings explained to both blacks and whites the just demands of black people.

Against this discouraging picture of revolt and conflict, important gains stood out. The black community was united in its own defense and proud of its achievements. Black history was studied, black poets and playwrights were celebrated, and ghetto blacks joined together to uplift their communities economically. Ten black men were elected to Congress, including one in the U.S. Senate. A black man sat on the Supreme Court, another on the Federal Reserve Board, and one was appointed to a presidential cabinet. Black mayors were elected in Cleveland, Ohio; Newark, New Jersey; Gary, Indiana; Washington, D.C.; and

Fayette, Mississippi. Civil rights laws were passed in 1964, 1965, and 1968, and these protected more than a million black voters in the South who went to polls by the end of the decade.

By 1970, 350 years after the first slaves were landed at Jamestown, the future of black America was still uncertain. Although more whites than ever before understood the evils of discrimination, the majority still did not. Although there was a greater desire to bring the American dream closer to reality, positive action came very slowly and often foundered on a white refusal to act against racism. Unfortunately, the growing black militancy and pride often tended to anger whites rather than to hasten racial justice. Despite some progress, not only were the prospects of achieving it unclear, but the effects of continued delay were frightening.

Bibliography

1. Joanne Grant, *Black Protest* (Fawcett, New York, 1968, paperback). Part 7 analyzes the political developments, and Part 8 discusses the economic developments in the black power movement, using source materials. An incomparable collection of views that should be used by teachers and students as supplementary reading and for basic research.

2. Stokely S. Carmichael and Charles V. Hamilton, *Black Power* (Vintage, New York, 1968, paperback), is a thorough discussion of the meaning and application of the term made famous by Carmichael. Useful for research by teachers and senior high school students.

3. August Meier and Elliott Rudwick, eds., *The Making of Black America* (Atheneum, New York, 1969, and paperback). Chapter 7 has a dozen articles by contemporary scholars on aspects of the black revolution—from black power to soul.

4. Julius Lester, *Look Out Whitey! Black Power's Gon' Get Your Mama* (Grove, New York, 1968, and paperback), is an insightful survey of various aspects of the black revolution as seen by an insider. Highly recommended to teachers and high school students for supplementary reading or research.

5. Floyd B. Barbour, ed., *The Black Power Revolt* (Porter Sargent, Boston, 1968, paperback), traces through documents the history of black power. For research by teachers and high school upperclassmen.

6. William Loren Katz, *Eyewitness: The Negro in American History* (Pitman, New York, 1967, and paperback). Chapter 20 discusses, through text, pictures, and eyewitness accounts, the white backlash, black power, and black progress.

7. C. Eric Lincoln, *Is Anybody Listening to Black America?* (Seabury Press, New York, 1968, paperback), is a potpourri of black and white comments on current racial developments. Could be helpful to teachers doing research, as well as high school upperclassmen.

8. Abraham Chapman, *Black Voices* (Mentor, New York, 1968, paperback), presents a wide range of writing by blacks, from Frederick Douglass to Darwin T. Turner. For teacher reference and student research.

9. Robert Canot, *Rivers of Blood, Years of Darkness* (Bantam, New York, 1967, paperback), is the story of the Watts riot of 1965, "the hate that hate produced." Useful for outside reading or research by teachers or high school students.

10. John A. Williams, *The Man Who Cried I Am* (Signet, New York, 1967, paperback), is a powerful novel of black life in America. Recommended to teachers and high school students as outside reading.

11. William H. Grier and Price M. Cobbs, *Black Rage* (Basic Books, New York, 1968, and Bantam paperback), is a controversial effort by two black psychiatrists to analyze the nature and roots of black rage in America. For teacher reference.

12. Martin Luther King, Jr., *Where Do We Go from Here: Chaos or Community?* (Beacon, Boston, 1967, paperback), is the civil rights leader's last book. It evaluates the white backlash and the black power movement. For research by teachers and students.

13. E. U. Essien-Udom, *Black Nationalism* (Dell, New York, 1962, paperback), is an interesting history of long-buried nationalistic impulses in black America. A useful reference for teachers.

14. Eldridge Cleaver, *Soul on Ice* (McGraw-Hill, New York, 1968, and paperback), expresses the Panther leader's argument that America's racism might well lead to America's end. Highly recommended for teachers and for students able to read it.

15. Jonathan Kozol, *Death at an Early Age* (Houghton Mifflin, Boston, 1967, and Bantam paperback), is a white teacher's story of how black children in Boston are crushed by the public school system. For outside reading and research by teachers and students.

16. Langston Hughes, *The Best of Simple* (Hill and Wang, New York, 1961, paperback), is a selection of essays on life cast in the words of Harlemite Jesse B. Semple. Excellent as outside reading on racial matters from a black urban viewpoint.

17. Dorothy Sterling, *Tear Down the Walls* (Doubleday, New York, 1968). Chapters 18 and 19 describe the black revolution of today in crisp prose, with fine pictures. Recommended as supplementary reading for students.

18. Gene Marine, *The Black Panthers* (Signet, New York, 1969, paperback), is the first book-length treatment of the militant black organization. For research by teachers.

19. *Report of the National Advisory Commission on Civil Disorders* (several paperback editions, 1968) is the famous Kerner Commission report. It should be used as a supplementary text in high school social studies classes, particularly in courses on Problems of American Democracy.

20. Hugh D. Graham and Ted Robert Gurr, eds., *The History of Violence in America* (Bantam, New York, 1969, paperback). Chapters 9, 10, 11, and 13 detail racial violence in America. For research.

21. *The Autobiography of Malcolm X* (Grove, New York, 1966, paperback) is the exciting story of the Negro leader who became the symbol of Black Nationalism. This powerful book is clear and stark, describing a life that seldom receives any attention or recognition in our schools. Recommended for teachers and high school students who wish to understand the background and development of this leader and of urban Negro ghettos.

22. Claude Brown, *Manchild in the Promised Land* (Macmillan, New York, 1965, and Signet paperback), is the story of a Harlem

youth who battled his way out of the New York ghetto. This frank and often brutal story can be usefully read by teachers and high school students.

23. Kenneth Clark, *Dark Ghetto* (Harper & Row, New York, 1965, and paperback), is the famous Negro social psychologist's description of the Negro ghettos, their origins and problems. It covers the political, social, economic, and cultural life of the urban ghetto. For teachers and high school upperclassmen doing research.

24. *Youth in the Ghetto* (A HARYOU-ACT publication, New York, 1963), is a careful, on-the-spot study of present conditions in Harlem. This historic document includes incisive statements by Harlem residents as well as important statistical tables. Part II, on education, employment, and problems of the black community, is particularly useful. Recommended for research by teachers and high school students.

25. John Williams, ed., *The Angry Black* (Lancer, New York, 1962, paperback), is composed of twelve stories and articles by writers expressing the angry mood of those facing discrimination. Among the contributors are James Baldwin, Ralph Ellison, Richard Wright, and editor John Williams.

26. Nathan Glazer and Daniel Patrick Moynihan, *Beyond the Melting Pot* (MIT Press, Cambridge, Mass., 1963, and paperback), discusses in Chapter One the problems New York blacks face: jobs, education, family life, housing, neighborhoods, leadership, and politics. Its penetrating analysis of this city's ethnic problems has significance for the entire nation. Recommended for teachers and the brightest upperclassmen.

27. C. Eric Lincoln, *The Black Muslims in America* (Beacon, Boston, 1961, and paperback), is the definitive study of this Black Nationalist movement. Recommended highly for teachers and high school students.

28. Mary Elizabeth Vroman, *Harlem Summer* (Putnam, New York, 1967), is a story about an Alabama teen-ager who spends a summer living and working in Harlem. Its central character is appealing, and the points raised are well worth class discussion. Highly recommended for junior high students.

29. Arthur M. Ross and Herbert Hill, eds., *Employment, Race and Poverty* (Harcourt, Brace & World, New York, 1967, paperback), is a thorough study of employment practices affecting the black worker. It consists of twenty essays by psychologists, economists, sociologists, historians, and educators. Recommended for teachers and high school seniors doing research.

30. Talcott Parsons and Kenneth B. Clark, eds., *The Negro American* (Houghton Mifflin, Boston, 1966, and paperback), is the most complete summary of our racial crisis available today. In thirty penetrating articles, noted authorities in each field dissect the components of the struggle for equal rights now taking place. Emphasis generally is on sociological and economic factors rather than political. Recommended for teachers and high school upperclassmen doing research.

31. August Meier and Elliott Rudwick, eds., *Black Protest in the Sixties* (Quadrangle Books, Chicago, 1970, paperback), is a readable chronicle drawn from the pages of the *New York Times,* with an articulate and concise summary of the decade by the editors. For teachers and high school students.

Chapter 4

SOURCES OF INEXPENSIVE
OR FREE MATERIALS

The number of sources of materials on the history of the Negro has been proliferating rapidly in recent years. The following is a partial list of places that may be contacted for various materials:

1. The Council on Interracial Books for Children, Inc., 9 E. 40th St., New York 10016, promotes books with interracial themes, supplies lists of materials for all school ages, and issues a useful newsletter.

2. The U.S. Government Printing Office, Washington, D.C., provides a catalog of available materials. Its inexpensive booklets and reports cover many aspects of this topic.

3. The U.S. Civil Rights Commission, Washington, D.C. Its annual report covers many phases of Negro life in America.

4. The New York State Commission Against Discrimination and similar organizations in many states provide reports and materials upon request.

5. The National Association for the Advancement of Colored People, 20 W. 40th St., New York 10018. The Association issues the monthly *Crisis* magazine, yearly reports, and a wide variety of booklets dealing with the Negro and civil rights.

6. The National Urban League, 14 E. 48th St., New York 10017, issues annual and special reports on opportunities for Negroes.

7. The Negro Bibliographic and Research Center, Inc., 117 R St., N.E., Washington, D.C., publishes a bimonthly bibliographic survey of materials on the Negro.

8. The American Civil Liberties Union, 156 Fifth Ave., New York 10010. Its newsletter and annual report devote space to civil rights issues involving Negroes.

9. The Citizens' Councils of America, Jackson, Miss. This headquarters of the White Citizens' Councils issues reports and booklets providing current anti-Negro viewpoints.

10. The Johnson Publishing Co., 1820 S. Michigan Ave., Chicago 60616, publishes *Ebony, Jet, Tan,* and *Negro Digest,* magazines devoted to Negro affairs and current events. Teachers desiring pictures will find *Ebony* particularly useful.

11. The Association for the Study of Negro Life and History, 1538 Ninth St., N.W., Washington, D.C., publishes the scholarly *Journal of Negro History* and the *Negro History Bulletin,* which is aimed at a wider audience of teachers and students. ASNLH provides both a catalog of its books and a catalog of hundreds of inexpensive pictures of Negro leaders, past and present.

12. *Muhammed Speaks,* 634 E. 79th St., Chicago 60619. This newspaper is the organ of the Black Muslim movement.

13. Anti-Defamation League of B'nai B'rith, 315 Lexington Ave., New York 10016. The ADL publishes a wide variety of booklets and materials on the Negro, civil rights, race relations, and related topics. It has a film library that provides movies and filmstrips at little or no cost. Catalogs of publications and of audio-visual materials are available free, on request.

14. Southern Regional Council, 5 Forsyth St., N.W., Atlanta, Ga. 30303, issues many booklets on the subject of race relations.

15. *Freedomways: A Quarterly Review of the Negro Freedom Movement,* by Freedomways Associates, 799 Broadway, New York City. Special issues are devoted to particular phases of the Negro revolution.

16. The Center for Urban Education, 33 W. 42nd St., New York 10036, publishes and distributes *The Negro in Schoolroom Literature* (Minnie W. Koblitz, editor), which offers an excellent array of books with complete annotations, for the earlier grades.

17. The Arno Press, 330 Madison Avenue, New York 10017, offers secondary schools a free kit of materials on Afro-American history and literature.

A Reading List of Books and Pamphlets on Race

(Anthropological and Scientific Approach)

Alpenfels, Ethel J., *Sense and Nonsense About Race,* New York, Friendship, 1957, paperback.

Anti-Defamation League Publications (Available from the Anti-Defamation League, 315 Lexington Ave., New York · 10016. Publications catalog sent on request.)

    Courlander, Harold, *On Recognizing the Human Species.*

    Goodman, Mary Ellen, *Race Awareness in Young Children.*

    Montagu, Ashley, *What We Know About "Race."*

    Tumin, Melvin M., ed., *Race and Intelligence.*

    Van Til, William, *Prejudiced—How Do People Get That Way?*

Benedict, Ruth, *Race: Science and Politics,* rev. ed., New York, Viking, 1959. Includes *The Races of Mankind.* (Also in paperback.)

Bernal, J. D., *Science in History,* New York, Cameron, 1954.

Brodrick, Alan Houghton, *Man and His Ancestry,* New York, Fawcett, 1964, paperback.

Count, Earl W., *This Is Race: An Anthology Selected from the International Literature in the Races of Man,* New York, Abelard-Schuman, 1950.

Dobzhansky, Theodosius, and L. C. Dunn, *Heredity, Race, and Society,* New York, Mentor, 1963, paperback.

Field, Henry, *The Races of Mankind,* New York, Hammond. (Map of Mankind, in full color.)

Hankins, Frank H., *The Racial Basis of Civilization: A Critique of the Nordic Doctrine,* New York, Knopf, 1926.

Howells, William, *Back of History,* New York, Doubleday, 1954.

Kluckhohn, Clyde, *Mirror for Man,* New York, Whittlesey, 1949. (Also in paperback.)

McWilliams, Carey, *Brothers Under the Skin,* Boston, Little, Brown, 1943. (Also in paperback.)

Montagu, Ashley, *Man's Most Dangerous Myth: The Fallacy of Race,* New York, Harper, 1952. (Also in paperback.)

UNESCO Publications, "The Race Question in Modern Science" Series, Paris, UNESCO, 1956. (Also available through UNESCO Publications Center, 317 E. 34th St., New York, N.Y. Also in paperback.)

Comas, Juan, *Racial Myths.*

Congar, Rev. Yves M. J., O.P., *The Catholic Church and the Race Question.*

Klineberg, Otto, *Race and Psychology.*

Dunn, L. C., *Race and Biology.*

Leiris, Michel, *Race and Culture.*

Lévi-Strauss, Claude, *Race and History.*

Little, Kenneth L., *Race and Society.*

Morant, G. M., *The Significance of Racial Differences.*

Rose, Arnold M., *The Roots of Prejudice.*

Shapiro, Harry L., *Race Mixture.*

U.S. Libraries with Negro History Book Collections*

1. Tuskegee Institute, Hollis Burke Frissell Library, Washington Collection, Tuskegee, Ala. 11,000 volumes.
2. Philander Smith College Library, 812 W. 13th St., Little Rock, Ark.
3. University of California (Santa Barbara), Wyles Collection, Goleta, Calif. 13,153 volumes. Emphasis primarily on the Negro as a slave, and implications of slavery and the Civil War.
4. Yale University Library, James Weldon Johnson Memorial Collection of Negro Arts and Letters, New Haven, Conn. Manuscripts and pictures.
5. Howard University Library, Negro Collection, Washington, D.C. 70,000 volumes.
6. Paine College, Warren A. Chandler Library, Augusta, Ga, 396 volumes. Shelf list only, especially on the race problem as it concerned churches in the Old South.
7. Fort Valley State College, Henry Alexander Hunt Memorial Library, Fort Valley, Ga. 861 volumes.
8. Savannah State College Library, Savannah, Ga. 1,000 volumes. Includes pamphlet and clipping file.
9. Johnson Publishing Company Library, 1820 S. Michigan Ave., Chicago, Ill. 2,500 volumes. Pictures, photostats, microfilm.
10. Dillard University Library, 2601 Gentilly Blvd., New Orleans, La. Card index on Negroes in New Orleans, from newspapers covering the period 1850-1865.

---

*Compiled by the American Federation of Teachers.

11. Xavier University Library, Palmetto and Pine St., New Orleans, La. Restricted use, closed August. Manuscripts, maps, pictures, photostats, microfilm.

12. Detroit Public Library, 5201 Woodward, Detroit, Mich. 849 volumes. Includes music, recordings, dance, drama.

13. St. Augustine Seminary Library, Divine Word Seminary, Bay St. Louis, Miss. 500 volumes. Maintained for missionary work among Negroes.

14. Rust College Library, Magee Memorial Library, Holly Springs, Miss. 3,659 volumes. Includes books by Negroes.

15. Tougaloo College, Eastman Library, Tougaloo, Miss.

16. Bronxville Public Library, 201 Pondfield, Bronxville, N.Y. Books presented in honor of Dr. Ralph J. Bunche by and about the Negro.

17. Columbia University Libraries, Special Collections, Alexander Gumby Collection, New York 10027.

18. New York Public Library Branch, Schomburg Collection, 103 W. 135th St., New York 10027. 33,500 volumes. A library of books, periodicals, manuscripts, clippings, pictures, prints, records, and sheet music which attempts to record the entire experience of people of African descent—historical and contemporary. Restricted use: materials must be used on the premises.

19. University of North Carolina, Louis Round Wilson Library, Chapel Hill, N.C.

20. Western Carolina College Library, Cullowhee, N.C.

21. Duke University Library, Durham, N.C.

22. Bennett College, Thomas F. Holgate Library, Greensboro, N.C. 1,481 volumes.

23. Richard B. Harrison Public Library, 214 S. Blount St., Raleigh, N.C. 3,500 volumes, Mimeographed bibliographies available.

24. The Rutherford B. Hayes Library, 1337 Hayes Ave., Fremont, Ohio. 65,000 volumes.

25. Wilberforce University, Carnegie Library, Daniel Alexander Payne Collection, Wilberforce, Ohio. 4,500 volumes. Includes manuscripts and pictures.

26. Lincoln University, Vail Memorial Library, Lincoln University, Penna. 2,900 volumes. Includes African materials.

27. The Free Library of Philadelphia, Social Science and History Department, Negro Collection, Logan Square, Philadelphia, Penna. 900 volumes.

28. Starks Library, Benedict College, Taylor and Harden St., Columbia, S.C. 29204. 28,100 volumes. Includes manuscripts, maps, pictures, slides.
29. Fisk University Library, Erastus Milo Cravath Memorial Library, Nashville, Tenn. 10,000 volumes. Includes manuscript collection. Restricted use: non-circulating.
30. Texas Southern University Library, Heartman Collection, 3201 Wheeler, Houston, Tex. 11,428 volumes. Includes maps and photographs.
31. Hampton Institute, Collis P. Huntington Memorial Library, George Foster Peabody Collection, Hampton, Va. 9,289 volumes.
32. Virginia State College Library, Norfolk Division, 2401 Corpew Ave., Norfolk, Va.
33. Virginia Union University, William J. Clark Library, 1500 Lombardy St., Richmond, Va. 1,650 volumes.

Museums of Negro History and Places of Interest*

Afro-American Institute, 14 John-Eliot Square, Roxbury, Massachusetts 02119.

Association for the Study of Negro Life and History (founded 1915), 1538 Ninth St., N.W., Washington, D.C., 20001. Mon.-Fri., 8:30-5.

John Brown House, 135 Main St., Red Bluff, Cailfornia 96080.

George Washington Carver National Monument (founded 1952), P.O. Box 38, Diamond, Missouri 64840. Daily, 8:30-5; closed Christmas. Admission free.

Chatham-Kent Museum (founded 1943; opened 1945), 59 William St. North, Chatham, Ontario, Canada. Tues., Thurs., Sat., 3-5, 7:30-9; first and third Sun., 3-5. Admission: adults, 25 cents; children, 10 cents; children accompanied by adults, free; group rates.

Sam Davis Memorial Association (founded 1927; opened 1930), Smyrna, Tennessee 37167. Mon.-Sat., 8-5; Sun., 1-5; closed Thanksgiving, Christmas. Admission: adults, 50 cents, children, 25 cents; group rates.

Fort Malden National Historic Park (founded 1941), 312 Laird Ave., Amherstburg, Ontario, Canada. Mon.-Sat., 9-8; Sun., 12-8 (July, Aug.); Mon.-Sat., 9-5; Sun., 1-5 (May, June, Sept.); Mon.-Sat., 10-4:30 (Oct.-Apr.); closed New Year's, Good Friday, Christmas. Admission free.

Frederick Douglass Home, 1411 W. St. S.E., Washington, D.C. 20018.

---

*Compiled in part by the American Federation of Teachers.

Frederick Douglass Institute of Negro Arts and History, 316-318 A Street, N.E., Washington, D.C. 20002. Mon.-Sun., 10-5:30. Admission free.

Dunbar House, 219 Summit St., Dayton, Ohio 45407. June-Sept. 15, weekends and holidays, 10-5; school groups by appointment, April-Sept. Admission: adults, 15 cents; children, 10 cents.

Hampton Institute, Hampton, Virginia 23368.

Lincoln-Tallman Museum (founded 1951), 440 North Jackson St., Janesville, Wisconsin 53545. May 15-Oct., Mon.-Sat., 9-5; Sun., 11-5. Admission: adults, 50 cents; children 12-18, 35 cents; under 12, 15 cents.

Museum of African-American History, 3806 S. Michigan Ave., Chicago, Illinois 60653. Daily, 1-5, including weekends; groups by appointment. Admission: adults, 50 cents; children, 25 cents.

The Museum for Black History and Culture, 392 Central Park West, New York, New York 10025.

The Old Slave Mart (founded 1938), 6 Chalmers St., Charleston, S.C. 29401. Mon.-Sat., 10-5 (winter); summer schedule varies; closed national holidays. Admission: museum, adults, 50 cents; children 6-12, 25 cents; art gallery, free.

Commodore Perry Memorial House and Dickson Tavern (opened 1963), 201 French St., Erie, Pennsylvania 16507. Sat., Sun., 1-4; June 15-Sept. 15, daily, 1-4. Admission: adults, 25 cents; children, 10 cents.

Rowland E. Robinson Memorial Association (founded 1937; opened 1963), Ferrisburg, Vermont 05456. June-Sept., daily, 8-8.

Colonel E. S. Robertson Home, U.S. Highway 81, Salado, Texas 76571. Mar. 15-June 15, Sept. 15-Oct. 15, Mon.-Sat., 10-5; Sun., 1:30-5; closed holidays. Admission: adults, 75 cents; children, 60 cents.

Soper Collection, Morgan State College, Baltimore, Maryland 21212.

Stowe House, 2950 Gilbert Ave., Cincinnati, Ohio 45206. June-Sept. 15, weekends and holidays, 9:30-5; school groups by appointment, April-Sept. Admission: adults, 15 cents; children, 10 cents; school groups with teacher, free.

Harriet Beecher Stowe House, 73 Forest St., Hartford, Connecticut 06105. Not open to the public.

Stratford Historical Society (founded 1925), 967 Academy Hill, Stratford, Connecticut 06497. Wed., Sat., Sun., 11-5 (May–Labor Day); Thurs., Fri., Sat., 1-5 (Labor Day–May 1); and by appointment. Admission: adults, 75 cents; children, 20 cents.

Tuskegee Institute, George Washington Carver Museum (founded 1938), P.O. Box 40, Tuskegee, Alabama 36083. Mon.-Sat., 10-4; Sun., 1-4; closed holidays. Admission free.

"Uncle Tom's Cabin" (founded 1948), Dresden, Ontario, Canada. April-Nov., daily, 10-sunset. Admission: adults, 50 cents; children, 10 cents; group rates.

University of Virginia, Orland E. White Research Arboretum (founded 1928), Boyce, Virginia 22670. By appointment. Admission free.

Zebulon B. Vance Birthplace (founded 1959; opened 1961), Reems Creek Road, Weaverville, North Carolina 28787. Tues.-Fri., 9-5; Sat., Sun., 2-5 (April-Oct.); Wed., 9-5; Sun., 2-5 (Nov.-March); closed Thanksgiving, Christmas, New Year's. Admission: adults, 25 cents; children, 10 cents.

Wallace House (opened 1897), 38 Washington Place, Somerville, New Jersey 08876. Tues.-Sat., 10-12, 1-5; Sun., holidays, 2-5; closed Thanksgiving, Christmas, New Year's. Admission: adults, 25 cents; children 5-12, 10 cents; school groups free.

Booker T. Washington National Monument (founded 1957; opened 1963), Virginia Route 122, 16 miles N.E. of Rocky Mount, Virginia 24151. Daily, 8-5; closed Christmas. Admission free.

Wilberforce University, Carnegie Library (founded 1953), Wilberforce, Ohio 45384. Mon., Tues., Thurs., Fri., 9-4; Wed., 9-11, 1-4; Sat., 9-12; Sun., 5-7:30; Mon.-Fri. eves., 6-9. Admission free.

Negro Art and Music

Atlanta University Gallery of Art, Atlanta, Georgia 30314.

Black Man's Art Gallery, San Francisco, California.

Cinque Gallery, Inc., 425 Lafayette St., New York, New York 10003. Tues.-Sat., 11-5; 7:30-9. Admission free.

Community Art Gallery, Brooklyn Museum, 188 Eastern Parkway, Brooklyn, New York 11238. Mon.-Sat., 10-5; Sun. and holidays, 1-5. Admission free.

Fisk Gallery of Art, Fisk University, Nashville, Tennessee 37103.

Howard University Gallery of Art (founded 1930), College of Fine Arts, 2455 Sixth St., N.W., Box 1023 (1), Washington, D.C. 20001. Mon.-Fri., 9-5; Sat., 10-12; closed holidays. Admission free.

Carl Murphy Fine Arts Center, Morgan State College, Baltimore, Maryland 21212.

Museum of African Art, Frederick Douglass Institute of Arts and History, 316-318 A Street, N.E., Washington, D.C. 20002. Mon.-Sat., 10-5:30. Admission free.

Museum of Afro-American History and Art, 3806 S. Michigan Ave., Chicago, Illinois 60653.

Museum of the National Center for Afro-American Artists, Roxbury, Massachusetts 02119.

New Orleans Jazz Museum (founded 1961), 1017 Dumaine St., New Orleans, Louisiana 70116. Tues.-Sat., and holidays, 10-5; Sun., 1-5; closed Christmas. Admission 25 cents.

Studio Gallery, Mt. Vernon, New York.

The Studio Museum in Harlem (founded 1968), 2033 Fifth Ave., New York, New York 10037. Mon. and Wed., 10-9; Thurs.-Fri., 10-6; Sat.-Sun., 1-6; closed Tues. Admission free.

Wayne State Art Gallery, Wayne State University, Detroit, Michigan 48102.

Index

Authors and Titles

Names